WHAT DOES CHILDHOOD TASTE LIKE?

WHAT DOES CHILDHOOD TASTE LIKE?

*Mental Workouts That Will Stretch, Bend, and Energize
the Way You Think, Respond, Dream, and Create*

Jack Maguire

A Stonesong Press Book

Quill
William Morrow
New York

Library of Congress Cataloging-in-Publication Data

Maguire, Jack.
    What does childhood taste like?

    "A Stonesong Press book."
    1. Intellect—Problems, exercises, etc.   2. Creative
thinking—Problems, exercises, etc.   I. Title.
BF431.3.M23   1986   153   86-12238
ISBN 0-688-06344-6 (pbk.)

Printed in the United States of America

First Edition

1 2 3 4 5 6 7 8 9 10

BOOK DESIGN BY ALLAN MOGEL

To Thomas Dale Cowan

Contents

WHAT DOES
CHILDHOOD
TASTE LIKE?

1
Introduction

Few of us have seen one, and it's not an attractive or impressive sight. It's about four inches wide, five inches long, and three inches high and is shaped like the meat from an oversized walnut. And yet it's the most complex and fascinating organism known to exist in the universe. Its products include the Pyramids of Giza, the alphabet, television, the *Mona Lisa,* the United States Constitution, French cuisine, baseball, the "Moonlight Sonata," and the New York Stock Exchange. We call this marvel a brain.

We each have a brain. It's our most valuable possession, but we tend to take it for granted, relying on it to function without any special treatment or care. The result is predictable. Despite our brain's astounding potential, we are continually dissatisfied with how it performs. Consider your mental life and how you'd like to improve it:

• Do you want to be more creative in your work? Your art? Your hobby? Your relationships?

• Do you want to make better decisions? Be more decisive? Respond more effectively to crises?

• Do you want to increase your ability to stay focused on a single task? To size up a situation accurately? To make better guesses?

• Do you want to retain more of what you learn? Recall specific information more easily? Recollect past events more vividly?

• Do you want to make mentally challenging tasks more enjoyable? Routine events more stimulating? Leisure moments more productive?

• Do you want to build your self-confidence? Become more aware of your potential? Nurture your talents?

• Do you want to overcome bad habits? Mental blocks? Obsessive worries? Stress triggers?

• Do you want to be able to express your feelings more successfully? Latch on to inspired thoughts before they slip away? Turn vague impressions into solid ideas? Capitalize on all that you've experienced?

When it comes to improving our bodies, we are pretty good at setting goals and developing activities to accomplish those goals. Chances are, you already do things to enhance your physical health, beauty, or strength. Maybe you play tennis, swim, jog, practice yoga, or do aerobics. Maybe you walk to work instead of ride. Maybe you take vitamins and avoid nicotine, salt, and caffeine. Maybe you foresake Fritos for fruit, black Russians for white wine, Pepsi for Perrier. But what about your brain? What do you do on a regular basis that will help you achieve the mental goals you want to achieve? What could you do?

The brain is like a muscle: The more effectively you exercise it, the better it performs. *What Does Childhood Taste Like?* is an original exercise program that helps you to give your mental muscle a good workout, conveniently and systematically. It equips you with enjoyable one-hour mind-stretching sets of activities that increase flexibility, memory, analytical powers, decision-making skills, and creativity.

For all the mystery surrounding the brain, during the last half century we have learned many things that underscore the value of a regular mental exercise program. The most important discovery is that cognitive ability—the ability to reason, solve problems, and invent—is acquired, not inborn. This means that we can train our mind to function more effectively; in fact, it won't function effectively at all unless we do. "The use-it-or-lose-it principle applies not only to the maintenance of physical flexibility, but to the maintenance of a high level of intellectual performance as well," says Dr. K. Warner Schaie, professor of human development at Pennsylvania State University. Neurologist Dr. Gardner Murphy phrases the same fact a bit more scientifically: "Uncultivated cortical functions diminish in strength when they are not used, much as muscles weaken when they are not exercised."

During our years of formal schooling, we're given a great deal of information, but little help in developing skills to process and apply that knowledge when we're out in the real world. We're trained to accomplish specific tasks to earn our living, but we are not trained to make general use of our mind to improve our life. Unless we take responsibility for ensuring that our brain gets ongoing stimulation in each major skill area, how can we be certain that we're not mentally stagnating? We may not be sharp enough to tell! In any event, we'll be at the mercy of our environment; and another fact that's been established about the brain is that our environment shapes the way we think.

We can see some startling implications of this fact when we examine recent "split-brain" studies. Physiological research has revealed distinct functional differences between the right and left hemispheres of the brain. Left-brain thinking utilizes our language skills and is associated with the development of logical, linear thought patterns that can be communicated verbally, both to ourselves and to others. Right-brain thinking, often called metaphoric thinking, employs our visual and spatial-recognition skills and characteristically manifests itself in terms of images, intuitive feelings, and artistic expression. We can talk about these images, feelings, and forms with the assistance of our left brain; but we can generate the images, feelings, and forms themselves only with our right brain.

Most of us today, at least in the Western world, are oriented toward logical, linear thinking (left brain); but our minds possess limitless resources for imaginative, intuitive thinking as well (right brain). These resources are liable to remain untapped unless we make a conscious effort to develop them by experimenting regularly with nonlogical, nonlinear mind activities.

Lawrence LeShan, a pioneer research psychologist, confirms that each of us needs to cultivate both modes of thinking—the rational and the imaginative—to make full use of the mind's potential. "The deepest goal," he states, "is to integrate the two in our lives, so that each viewpoint is heightened and sharpened by the knowledge of the other."

Recently, cognitive scientists have made an even more revolutionary discovery about the workings of the brain. They have demonstrated that the structure of brain cells can actually change, becoming more complex and more capable of generating intelligence given the stimulation of an enriched environment, such as a continually challenging series of mental development activities. In other words, our brain may be even more like a muscle than we once imagined: It may literally, as well as figuratively, grow with exercise.

The cerebral cortex of the brain contains about ten billion neuron cells that assist in processing thoughts. Our overall mental capability is based not so much on the number of neurons in our brain as on the number of connections among these neurons. A single neuron can possess as many as ten thousand connective links with other cells or almost none. A single neuron can be directly and indirectly linked with a network of up to six hundred thousand other neurons. These links and the patterns of energy transit that they can create are what make up our intellectual ability: the more links, the greater that ability.

In experiments conducted in the United States and Argentina over the past two decades, cognitive scientists took a pool of genetically equal laboratory rats and divided them into three groups. The first group was confined to plain wire cages, three to a cage. This was labeled a standard environment. The second group was placed in isolation, each rat in a separate cage consisting of three opaque walls, one transparent wall, dim lights, and little chance for outside stimulation. This was labeled an impoverished environment. The third group was divided into "play teams" of ten to twelve rats, and each team was housed in a large, brightly lit, multilevel cage filled with a variety of toys. This was labeled an enriched environment.

After different periods of time in different experimental runs (ranging from a few days to several months), the researchers presented the rats in each group with a number of standard laboratory tests for intelligence, such as maze running. The rats from the enriched environment were consistently more intelligent and quicker to learn.

The researchers then removed and studied the brains of the rats. In all cases, the rats from the enriched environment had thicker cortical layers and heavier brains, due to an increase in the size and complexity of individual neurons, which had developed considerably more connective links to other neurons than the neurons of the rats from the standard and impoverished environments. The researchers also found that it made no difference whether the rats were old or young: The results were the same.

What do these studies have to say about our own mental development? Before these experiments, the scientific community believed that the brain reached a final stage of development during adolescence and did not change structurally thereafter, except, perhaps, to deteriorate during old age. These new experiments totally contradict that conception. According to Michael Hutchinson, who describes the experiments in detail in his book *Megabrain:*

> When we use the fruits of this research to think about the human brain, with its much more powerful and important cortex, it makes sense that humans who are exposed to enriched environments—that is, humans whose brains are challenged and stimulated—should experience changes in the shape, size and structure of the cortex. These changes should result in enhanced cortical function, including increased intelligence, creativity and so on. Very short exposures to stimulation can bring about these changes. That is, it's likely that short periods of intense brain stimulation can increase brain complexity and capacity for humans of any age.

Based on research with doctors, therapists, educators, decision-makers, and creativity experts, *What Does Childhood Taste Like?* enables you to give your brain the enriched environment it needs to grow more powerful. Activities similar in content, structure, or purpose to many of the exercises in this book have been used for years by people in all walks of life to improve their mental performance.

In the business world, mind-expanding techniques practiced in think tanks, brainstorming sessions, and creativity seminars have yielded impressive results. Executives of one company, seeking to find a way to pack, distribute, and sell potato chips more compactly without crushing them, engaged in guided associations. They thought about nature and what in nature reminded them of potato chips. This led them to consider dry leaves, which, when they are moistened, pack together tightly without crumbling. Pursuing this image, they came up with the idea for Pringles, a landmark in food packaging. A consultant to a farm-products company interested in making sure that its seeds were planted properly began by thinking of a machine gun and wound up imagining a roll of biodegradable tape containing properly spaced seeds that could be easily laid in an open furrow. After 3M failed to market a bra made of nonwoven fiber, a company employee realized in the course of a mental exercise that the shape of the cups would be perfect for surgical masks; now 3M has a new mask division with annual sales of more than $25 million.

Athletes, keenly aware of the value of physical conditioning, are among the most enthusiastic advocates of mental exercise. Lee Evans, four-hundred-meter Olympic medalist and world recordholder in 1968, attributes his success to memory training. He rehearsed every race mentally based on the sensations he had experienced and the data he had acquired during previous runs. During these rehearsals, Evans comments, he concentrated on remembering and analyzing the smallest details he could, "searching out and correcting weaknesses in every step I took." Quarterback Fran Tarkenton trained himself repeatedly before games by "running whole blocks of plays in my head . . . trying to visualize every game situation, every defense they could throw at me." The results, he claims, were not only improved performance during competition, but also a greater personal enjoyment of the sport.

Most artists depend on a whole range of mental exercises to elicit ideas and give form to their inspirations. Playwright Tennessee Williams routinely played a game by himself of arbitrarily casting someone he knew into a situation described in the daily newspaper. One such game helped him to create the character of Blanche DuBois in *A Streetcar Named Desire*. Novelist Joyce Carol Oates regularly sets aside a quiet time for scribbling her thoughts in a special style of longhand that includes code words and phrasing no one else can decipher. Singer Stevie Wonder works with metaphors to trigger song possibilities. Actress Linda Hunt has a personal way of studying paintings to recharge her mental energies.

What Does Childhood Taste Like? helps you to help yourself. You may have a specific goal you wish to achieve by exercising your mind—bolstering your willpower, generating a million-dollar idea, becoming a better conversationalist, avoiding manipulation by others, revitalizing your interest in your profession. Or instead of killing a few hours a week, you may just want to make them live.

The chief value of any exercise program does not necessarily lie in the specific, tangible results you can count on achieving if you follow the program faithfully. Instead, it lies in a general improvement of the overall quality of your life—an improvement that may be so subtle that it escapes your conscious awareness until one glorious moment when it catches you by surprise and convinces you that the time spent exercising was well invested. For years I've lifted weights, jogged, and played racquetball fairly regularly. I could feel my muscles getting stronger, I could see my game improving, but every now and then—especially when I'd be pressed for time and tempted to skip a workout—I'd say to myself, "Do I really need to keep building my body this way? Couldn't I lead a perfectly fine, healthy life without all this extra stuff?" Then one day last summer I found myself alone on miles of beach. Without a second's thought I began running, leaping, and jumping out of sheer exuberance. For over an hour I felt complete freedom, ease, and comfort, despite how much I was exerting myself. It was one of the most rewarding experiences I've ever had, but it would have been impossible if I hadn't kept up those years of exercise.

In the case of the mind, the same type of benefit can occur, thanks to regular exercise. I hope this book brings you many moments of uninhibited brilliance and joy.

How to Use *What Does Childhood Taste Like?*

The core of *What Does Childhood Taste Like?* is five chapters of original exercises. Each chapter concentrates on a key area of mental skills.

Flexibility—the ability to generate abstract ideas from concrete details, and vice versa; to interpret experience literally as well as metaphorically and symbolically; to draw illuminating analogies; and to open passageways between dream consciousness and waking consciousness

Memory—the ability to retain and recall facts, figures, and faces quickly and accurately to translate unfamiliar data into more recognizable terms; and to reconstruct past experiences vividly

Analysis—the ability to make reasonably accurate estimates; to form practical hypotheses; to separate a whole into its parts; and to detect significant patterns and relationships among diverse items

Decision-making—the ability to make effective and informed judgments; to establish objectives, priorities, and procedures; and to respond successfully to anticipated and unanticipated events

Creativity—the ability to entertain contrasting and opposite points of view at the same time; to invent fresh and imaginative approaches to problems and opportunities; to think in nonlinear, atypical ways; and to express sensations and intuitions freely and coherently

Each chapter consists of a psych-up to prepare you for the exercises, several exercises that can be performed individually or serially, and a mind-play section that outlines mental games you can play based on the skills you've developed. Every exercise is followed by adaptations and related exercises, so you can repeat the same kind of exercise in succeeding workouts. At the end of each chapter, other exercises are listed, giving you alternative activities in the same skill area.

Some exercises can be repeated innumerable times with fresh rewards. Some can be prototypes for creating your own exercises. Some lead to interaction with other people, either by suggesting teamwork on the activity itself or by preparing you to derive more stimulation from just being around people—observing them, talking with them, and listening to them.

All the exercises take as their starting point your experiences, points of view, memories, or knowledge. They will activate your mind no matter what your educational background, profession, culture, beliefs, or lifestyle.

What Does Childhood Taste Like? also has a preliminary chapter of relaxation and concentration techniques. You can use these techniques to limber up your mind before an exercise session or whenever you feel the need to compose yourself during the day. They will help you achieve those mental states of being that are the most productive.

The next to last section, "Superfitness," offers guidelines for going beyond a regular mind fitness program to self-determined long-range mentally demanding projects. It presents models for life/work planning as well as ideas for pursuing new fields of knowledge, overcoming bad habits and developing good ones, and increasing the benefits of the activities that are inextricable parts of the way you live.

What Does Childhood Taste Like? is a very flexible program that you can easily customize to fit your personal objectives and schedule. Each chapter and each exercise stands on its own. Described below is a complete program, followed by some alternatives.

The Complete Program

To obtain the full benefits of the program, it is best to do each exercise as you encounter it. The average time necessary to complete each exercise is about ten minutes in the chapters that focus on flexibility and memory and about fifteen minutes in the chapters that focus on analysis, decision-making, and creativity. So each chapter has about one hour's worth of exercises—just enough time to give your brain an effective workout without becoming fatigued.

Here are instructions for following the complete program:

1. Do the self-assessment exercise "Your Mental Check-up."

2. Read the section "Mind Conditioning: Relaxation and Concentration Techniques."

3. Experiment with one of the activities under the headings "Meditation," "Visualization," or "Contemplation." Because all of these activities have the same purpose—to achieve a state of relaxation and concentration—it is a good idea to limit yourself to one or two at a time. So plan to return to this section from time to time until you have mastered all the activities.

4. Read one chapter of the book at a single sitting, performing each exercise in the chapter as you go along. Set aside a time during the day when you will be free from distraction for at least an hour, and choose a spot where you can think comfortably. Since some of the exercises require paper and pencil or pen, you also want a spot where you can write comfortably. Consider creating a separate notebook (ideally, loose-leaf, divided according to the exercise categories) in which you can record your responses to exercises as well as any thoughts on the topic at hand.

5. When you have completed all the exercises in the book, return to the first chapter and devote a single session to performing selected activities from the "More Workouts" feature that appears after each original exercise. Drawing on these activities, along with those described in the "More Exercises" feature at the end of each chapter, you can sustain your mental fitness program for as long as you wish. Attached to each exercise are suggestions for making individual exercise sessions progressively more challenging.

6. After three months of fairly regular mental exercise sessions (at least once a week), read and complete the "Training Progress Report" section at the end of this book. You can continue to return to this section every three months.

Alternatives to the Complete Program

The options for an effective mental fitness program are as varied as the minds that read this book. You can create your own program simply by regularly doing a few of the activities in this book.

Here are some basic principles to follow in creating your own mental fitness program:

• Plan to act. Such planning can range from telling yourself that you will do "some exercises each weekend" to drawing up your own schedule of specific exercises you will do at specific times.

• Work toward achieving a consistent duration, structure, and quality in your exercise sessions. Devote the same amount of time to each session. Try to follow the same basic order of events in each session. One way to ensure that you do this is to lend a degree of ceremony or ritual to each session. You may, for example, want to begin by using a relaxation or concentration technique and conclude by making a few notes on how the session went.

• Keep track of your progress. Every now and then, assess your performance in the program. Ask yourself: "How have I benefited from the program?" "What do I still need to do?" "What would I like to have happen as a result of the program?" "How can I help this happen?"

Here are just a few of the many possible alternate ways of using *What Does Childhood Taste Like?*:

• Pick one exercise from each chapter to perform in a single session.

• Copy one of the exercises and its related activities (from "More Workouts" and "More Exercises") on a piece of paper. Put it someplace where you will see it frequently during the day. From time to time over the next week or month, try out different items listed on the paper, either specifically as the book directs or in whatever ways you choose. Change the paper every week or month.

• Set up a plan with a partner. Ask a family member or a friend or a group of friends either to join you on a regular basis in performing exercises or to agree to perform exercises on a regular basis simultaneously with you and keep you informed periodically about the results.

• Pick one chapter and spend a lot of time on it. Over the course of a month or two, perform as many of the activities described in the chapter as you conveniently can, drawing from the exercises themselves and the "More Workouts" and "More Exercises" sections. When you are satisfied that you have made sufficient progress with the material in that chapter, move on to another.

Your Mental Check-up

Before you start your program, you need to take a look at how fit your mind is right now. These questions will give you a general profile of your "mental fitness."

This check-up is not a precise instrument. It elicits your opinions about your mental abilities and habits rather than objectively measuring them. But when it comes to judging how effectively you think, your own opinions are the most revealing and valuable source of information.

The main purpose of the check-up is to start you wondering and, eventually, thinking about how you use your mind's potential. This kind of ongoing self-evaluation will help you monitor your progress as you continue your mental fitness program and help you apply what you learn toward making your life more efficient and satisfying.

After you've pursued your program for three months, get another check-up using the "Training Progress Report" section at the end of the book. Your original score is not nearly as meaningful as the difference between it and the score you give yourself after a sustained period of exercise.

The check-up below has two parts. First, you'll find your mental fitness score, then you'll have a chance to tackle some open-ended questions about your opinions and experiences regarding mental fitness.

Part One

Circle the number next to the word or phrase that best describes your situation. Do not circle more than one number per statement, and be sure to complete each statement. Then, for each category, add the circled numbers and divide this total by the number of statements to get your category rating. When you've finished all the categories, add the category ratings and divide by the number of categories for your total mental fitness score. Estimate all totals to at least two decimal points.

Category 1

1. I consciously use word pictures—metaphors and analogies—to communicate more clearly:

1 rarely
2 occasionally
3 about half the time
4 most of the time
5 continually

2. I consciously use word pictures—metaphors and analogies—to make what others are communicating clearer to myself:

1 rarely
2 occasionally
3 about half the time
4 most of the time
5 continually

3. I can identify specific images that I use repeatedly when communicating with others:

1 not at all
2 with much difficulty
3 with some difficulty
4 fairly easily
5 very easily

4. I remember my nightly dreams:

1 rarely
2 occasionally
3 about half the days
4 most days
5 almost every day

5. I make a conscious effort to understand my dreams:

1 rarely
2 occasionally
3 about half the time
4 most of the time
5 continually

6. I record my experiences and/or impressions:

1   rarely
2   occasionally
3   fairly regularly
4   very often
5   almost every day

7. I can articulate my feelings:

1   not at all
2   with much difficulty
3   with some difficulty
4   fairly easily
5   very easily

SUM OF NUMBERS CIRCLED: _____
CATEGORY RATING (sum divided by 7): _____

Category 2

1. I remember my childhood:

1   very poorly
2   somewhat poorly
3   fairly well in the case of major incidents
4   fairly well in the case of most incidents
5   very vividly

2. I recall names of people and places after first exposure:

1   rarely
2   occasionally
3   about half the time
4   most of the time
5   continually

3. I use written notes to remember items:

1   continually
2   most of the time
3   about half the time
4   occasionally
5   rarely

4. I employ special tricks to remember things:

1   rarely
2   occasionally
3   about half the time
4   most of the time
5   continually

5. I use _____ special trick(s) routinely to remember things:

1   no
2   one
3   two or three
4   several
5   many

6. I find myself forgetting things on my schedule:

1   continually
2   most of the time
3   about half the time
4   occasionally
5   rarely

7. I typically recall facts about a subject:

1   in general terms
2   with a small amount of detail
3   in a fair amount of detail
4   in substantial detail
5   in very specific detail

8. I find myself looking up the same one phone number or the same one fact:

1   continually
2   most of the time
3   about half the time
4   occasionally
5   rarely

SUM OF NUMBERS CIRCLED: _____

CATEGORY RATING (sum divided by 8): _____

Category 3

1. I estimate time lengths of events:

1   very poorly
2   inaccurately most of the time
3   inaccurately about half the time
4   accurately most of the time
5   with a great degree of accuracy

2. I estimate distances between two points:

1   very poorly
2   inaccurately most of the time
3   inaccurately about half the time
4   accurately most of the time
5   with a great degree of accuracy

3. I estimate weights and sizes:

1   very poorly
2   inaccurately most of the time
3   inaccurately about half the time
4   accurately most of the time
5   with a great deal of accuracy

4. I solve puzzles and mysteries:

1   with a great deal of difficulty most of the time
2   with some degree of difficulty most of the time
3   with some degree of difficulty about half the time
4   with ease most of the time
5   with ease all of the time

5. I am able to anticipate the outcome of events:

1   rarely
2   occasionally
3   about half the time
4   most of the time
5   continually

6. I employ special tricks to analyze things:

1   rarely
2   occasionally
3   about half the time
4   most of the time
5   continually

7. I use _____ special trick(s) routinely to analyze things:

1   no
2   one
3   two or three
4   several
5   many

SUM OF NUMBERS CIRCLED: _____

CATEGORY RATING (sum divided by 7): _____

Category 4

1. I respond to crises:

1   with a great deal of failure and frustration
2   with failure and frustration most of the time
3   with failure and frustration about half the time
4   with success and comfort most of the time
5   with success and comfort all of the time

2. I formulate specific and measurable objectives for a project:

1   rarely
2   occasionally
3   about half the time
4   most of the time
5   continually

3. I establish priorities among different goals and tasks:

1   rarely
2   occasionally
3   about half the time
4   most of the time
5   continually

4. I experiment with alternatives when performing a task or achieving a goal:

1   rarely
2   occasionally
3   about half the time
4   most of the time
5   continually

5. I employ specific procedures in order to come to decisions:

1 rarely
2 occasionally
3 about half the time
4 most of the time
5 continually

6. I use _____ specific procedure(s) routinely to come to decisions:

1 no
2 one
3 two or three
4 several
5 many

7. I have trouble coming to a final decision:

1 continually
2 most of the time
3 about half the time
4 occasionally
5 rarely

SUM OF NUMBERS CIRCLED: _____
CATEGORY RATING (sum divided by 7): _____

Category 5

1. I experience what I consider to be a creative thought:

1 rarely
2 occasionally
3 fairly regularly
4 very often
5 all of the time

2. I act on the creative thoughts I experience:

1 rarely
2 occasionally
3 about half the time
4 most of the time
5 continually

3. I employ specific procedures to inspire creative thoughts:

1   rarely
2   occasionally
3   fairly regularly
4   very often
5   all of the time

4. I use _____ specific procedure(s) routinely to inspire creative thoughts:

1   no
2   one
3   two or three
4   several
5   many

5. I entertain myself in leisure moments by inventing my own activities to perform:

1   rarely
2   occasionally
3   about half the time
4   most of the time
5   continually

6. I have trouble coming up with innovative approaches to things:

1   continually
2   most of the time
3   about half the time
4   occasionally
5   rarely

SUM OF NUMBERS CIRCLED: _____
CATEGORY RATING (sum divided by 6): _____

MENTAL FITNESS SCORE (sum of category ratings divided by 5): _____

Category 1 gives a profile of your flexibility; 2, memory; 3, analytical powers; 4, decision-making skills; 5, creativity. The closer to a score of 5 you come, the more mentally fit you have rated yourself.

Part Two

Category 1: Flexibility

1. To me, "mental flexibility" means:

_____

_____

_____

_____

2. Ways in which I am mentally flexible are:

_____

_____

_____

_____

3. Ways in which I need to be more mentally flexible are:

_____

_____

_____

_____

4. Specific things I can do to develop my mental flexibility are:

_____

_____

_____

_____

Category 2: Memory

1. To me, having a good memory means:

_____

_____

_____

_____

2. Ways in which I use my memory well are:

_____

_____

_____

_____

3. Ways in which I need to use my memory more effectively are:

_____

_____

_____

_____

4. Specific things I can do to develop a better memory are:

_____

_____

_____

_____

Category 3: Analysis

1. To me, being good at analyzing things means:

_____

_____

_____

_____

2. Ways in which I analyze things well are:

_____

_____

_____

_____

3. Ways in which I need to be better in analyzing things are:

_____

_____

_____

_____

4. Specific things I can do to develop my analytical abilities are:

_____

_____

_____

_____

Category 4: Decision-making

1. To me, effective decision-making means:

_____

_____

_____

_____

2. Ways in which I am good at making decisions are:

_____

_____

_____

_____

3. Ways in which I need to become better at decision-making are:

_____

_____

_____

_____

4. Specific things I can do to develop my decision-making abilities are:

_____

_____

_____

_____

Category 5: Creativity

1. To me, "mental creativity" means:

_____

_____

_____

_____

2. Ways in which I am creative are:

_____

_____

_____

_____

3. Ways in which I need to become more creative are:

_____

_____

_____

_____

4. Specific things I can do to develop my creative abilities are:

_____

_____

_____

_____

Mind Conditioning: Relaxation and Concentration Techniques

You face a difficult thinking challenge. You need to write a report, to reorganize your budget, to study for an examination, to decide what to do about a disagreement with your mate, or to remember where you stashed last year's Halloween costume. You furrow your brow, you clench your fingers, you press your tongue against your upper lip, and you silently shout to the central command officer of your brain: "Set your mind to it!"

The directive "set your mind to it" conjures up the same kind of image as "put your nose to the grindstone, your shoulder to the wheel, and your ear to the ground." We think about mental work the same way we think about physical work. When we are unable to produce on demand a "correct" response to a situation, we borrow a term from locomotion and say we are "blocked" or a term from sod-busting and say we are "stumped" or a term from ophthalmology and say we are "stymied." We long for a "breakthrough," an "uprooting," a "revelation."

The body and the mind *are* linked together and influence each other. When we feel pressured to perform a mental task, our heart beats faster, our breathing rate increases, our muscles stiffen, and the adrenaline level in our blood goes up. These physical developments, however, are not preconditions to better thinking. They are merely symptoms that we are feeling pressure.

Many people are convinced that they function best under pressure, and they are probably right, but the reason for this is not because pressure stimulates the mind to work "harder." Pressure is more likely, in fact, to make it "harder" for the brain to work. We are all tempted occasionally to associate success with pressure. When we are under pressure, we are more conscious of the act of thinking—something we are actually doing all the time—and we are guaranteed a tangible product for our thoughts, whether it is an actual accomplishment or only an indelible memory of a mentally engaging experience.

In times of pressure, fixed goals are imposed on our labors and external forces offer strong pleasure-and-pain incentives for us to come up with results within a given number of hours, days, weeks, or months. We produce these results, usually. And record them, usually. And the record impresses us. But the results we have produced may or may not be the best results we are capable of producing.

Unfortunately, by allowing external come-and-go pressure patterns to determine how, when, and why we think, we can turn ourselves into "reactors" instead of "actors," and our mental efforts will be marked by the pains of coercion rather than the pleasures of voluntary release. We will wait to be prodded or "turned on" before we do any independent thinking.

One thing that mental activity and physical activity certainly do have in common is that we tend to perceive each in terms of mechanical activity. We regard the mind and body as machines that are the means to a variety of ends and that are either "on" or "off." We seldom think about the body unless it "malfunctions" or we experience difficulty applying it to a specific task or it surprises us with a particularly strong response to an outside stimulus. Similarly, we give little attention to the mind unless it fails to compute a right answer in a test situation or shifts us unexpectedly into an undesired mood or delivers an especially imaginative idea seemingly out of nowhere or simply seems to stop, leaving us stranded and bored.

Like machines, the mind and body operate according to principles of cause and effect: Something is set in motion and there's a result. But unlike machines, they are living organisms. They require attention, nurturing, and cultivation rather than inspection, repair, and remodeling.

Physical conditioning is based on listening to the body and learning how to respect and facilitate its dynamic capabilities. Mental conditioning is based on listening to the mind, getting in tune with its natural rhythms, and cooperating with these rhythms to make better use of the mind's potential. The starting point for both types of conditioning is the mastery of the art of relaxation and concentration.

None of us has any trouble admiring and appreciating the ability to relax and concentrate, but we find it difficult to develop relaxation and concentration skills. We are accustomed to performing logical activities that are directly aimed toward achieving specific goals. We insist on being "rational" and strain to reach "the right answer"—the sooner the better. The methods and rewards of relaxation and concentration training are much more subtle, nonlinear, and long-range.

Even the concepts behind the words *relaxation* and *concentration* are subtle. Could we define them in precise, rational terms if we were playing a game called Dictionary at a party? We would probably provide examples, hoping that they would substitute for definitions.

Because we so often associate mental activities with mechanical activities, we might portray relaxation and concentration as opposites. We would describe relaxation as watching television or sunbathing or having a cup of coffee. *Relaxation* would appear to mean "time out" or "not having to think about anything in particular." We would describe concentration as sitting hunched over a desk and staring intently at the printed page in front of us or pacing back and forth as we mentally scan the same body of information over and over again. *Concentration* would appear to mean "work time" or "forcing oneself to think about one thing in particular."

The truth is that relaxation and concentration are inextricably bound up with each other, like yin and yang, heartbeat and heartrest. They operate together to make both our time out and our work time more profitable and enjoyable.

Relaxation involves achieving a mental state of calmness and balance that is physiologically the most refreshing, the most receptive to learning, and the most conducive to inspiration. Our heart rate drops, our breathing becomes more regular, and our brain begins to emit steadier wave patterns. But to accomplish this state, we must be able to concentrate on keeping an open mind: resisting distractions and counteracting the flight-or-fight impulse that bids us to do something—anything—in response to whatever we experience.

Concentration involves controlling and centering our mental energies so that at a given moment we can select what we want to think about and focus on it clearly and steadily for as long as we wish. But to accomplish this, we need to be able to relax our conscious busy-ness, detaching our mind from peripheral concerns and cravings. If we trust in our mind's natural tendency toward equilibrium, it will give us the peace that will let us commit ourselves to the moment at hand.

Relaxation-concentration is a unified, dynamic process. Techniques for listening to the mind tend to incorporate aspects of both relaxation and concentration and include procedures that are physical as well as mental. As a result, phrases attempting to describe these techniques often seem paradoxical—*passive concentration, active relaxation*—precisely because our rational mind is inclined to categorize items in an either-or fashion: the mind as opposed to the body, work as opposed to play, the real as opposed to the imaginary.

Certain relaxation and concentration techniques, for all their simplicity and effectiveness, can seem mighty strange in practice. Leonard Bernstein frequently rests on the floor to induce what he calls a "twilight state of consciousness, similar to the state of mind which immediately precedes sleep," during which he can experience creative visions. "Many a time," Bernstein remarks, "my wife has walked into my studio and found me lying down and has said, 'Oh, I thought you were working, excuse me!' And I was working, but you'd never have known it."

When Atlee Hammaker, the pitcher for the San Francisco Giants, faces a particularly tense moment during a game, he may walk to the edge of the mound and stand stock-still for several moments. Its appears as if he is not doing anything. But he is doing something very critical to his performance. He is relaxing and concentrating at the same time by breathing from his physical center of gravity, the point about an inch or two below the navel that the Japanese call *hara*.

As you begin to practice relaxation and concentration techniques, you may feel peculiar at first. In that case, remind yourself that it is the "peculiarity" of these disciplines that makes them valuable, for they work to counteract habitual patterns of stress and neglect, to transcend typical modes of perception, attention, and awareness, and to make you familiar in entirely new ways with the special powers of the mind in general and your mind in particular.

The relaxation and concentration techniques offered below are adapted from various schools of mind discipline and are specially designed to supplement the mental fitness exercises that form the body of this book. Applying one or more of these techniques before each exercise session will help prepare your mind to function more efficiently and effectively during each exercise. Performed regularly, these techniques will enable you to increase your self-control and attain higher degrees of conscious awareness. As you experiment with different techniques over a period of time, you will find those that work best for you.

The techniques are grouped into three divisions. Under the title "Meditation" are techniques for developing your general powers of receptivity and awareness. Under the title "Visualization" are techniques for developing your powers to form mental images. Under the title "Contemplation" are techniques for developing your powers of pure, nongoal-oriented thinking.

Meditation

To those of us who came of age during the 1960s, meditation seemed to be a newly unearthed, drug-free means of inducing an altered state of consciousness, imported to the Western world by Indian gurus who had been doing it on top of mountains for centuries but who had remained unknown until television made the world smaller and brought them into our living rooms.

There is a kernel of truth in this scenario. For hundreds of years, the Western world has engaged in similar psychic disciplines: Prayer in the Judeo-Christian tradition can produce roughly equivalent states of consciousness, and there is much in the spiritual exercises of St. Ignatius that is analagous to the teachings of Maharishi Mahesh Yogi. But it was the popularization of Eastern philosophies during the 1960s that forced the average Westerner to redefine *meditation.*

In the Western world prior to this time, meditation had come to mean mental rumination or pondering geared toward improving one's understanding of a particular concept or field of knowledge. The Eastern notion of meditation is less influenced by practical issues and much more sharply focused on transforming an individual's psychological and physiological state of mind. The widespread introduction of Eastern meditational practices into Western popular culture helped Westerners discover that meditation could help one realize and develop one's general powers of attention and awareness.

Asked for a definition of *meditation* that synthesized both Western and Eastern attitudes, American poet and Zen enthusiast Gary Snyder called it "the process of learning to do one thing at a time." Arturo Toscanini was an early and ardent practitioner of this kind of meditation, and he frequently credited it with opening his mind to a wider and richer range of experiences. When the conductor was eighty, his son asked him what he considered to be his most significant achievement. He replied, "Whatever I happen to be doing at the moment is the biggest thing in my life, whether I am conducting a symphony or peeling an orange."

The ultimate benefits of regular meditation are:

• Meditation allows your brain to operate free from the constraints and pitfalls of rational thought systems. It reasserts your brain's normal functioning much as sleep does, so that it can respond effectively to each new challenge.

• Meditation strengthens and develops your patience, clear-headedness, and "mindfulness" by encouraging the exercise of your natural powers of discipline.

• Meditation breaks down artificial barriers between the body and the mind imposed by your normal consciousness. It encourages the cooperation of your mind and body in everyday task performance.

• Meditation expands your experiential knowledge of how your mind performs. It works to give you confidence that you do have limitless capacities for mental growth and that you can exercise increased control over your mental and physical states.

• Meditation builds channels between your conscious mind and your unconsicous mind, putting you more in touch with your intuition and helping you to validate it.

• Meditation enables you to reach what Buddha called *bhavana* and what Albert Einstein called operational thoughtfulness. It cleanses your mind of destructively repetitive or circular thinking habits, ill will, delusions, restlessness, and nonproductive appetites and helps you live fully in the present.

The techniques that follow will enable you to begin experiencing on your own this transcendent awareness. Before using one of the techniques, read it several times, until you can easily remember each step. Then assume a comfortable but alert position. Most people find that the best position is lying on a hard surface, face up, the legs spread about a foot apart, and the arms turned palm upward about a foot from either leg. If it is more convenient or desirable, you can sit in a chair with your back as straight as is comfortable, your arms held loosely against your sides, your hands placed either palm upward or downward on your legs, your legs bent at a right angle, and your feet placed firmly on the floor. "Pretend," as the poet Allen Ginsberg recommends, "that your head is balancing the sky and your feet are pushing roots into the ground."

While you are performing a relaxation and concentration technique, you may find your mind wandering. Do not fight it. Simply let any thoughts or impressions run across your mind and gently lead your mind back to the meditation. As you become more familiar and comfortable with a technique, you can expand the amount of time you spend performing it, until you reach an ideal time of ten to fifteen minutes per technique.

Technique 1

Close your eyes. Concentrate on your forehead. Without moving it, notice how it feels. Do not try to put your impression into words; simply note the feeling itself. Imagine there is a glowing light there. Relax your forehead. Feel it expanding as it gives in to gravity. Then slowly move the light down to the area around your eyes. Note how that area feels. Relax that area. Feel it expanding as it gives in to gravity.

Continue this process, moving down to your nose area, then your mouth area, then your jaw area. Move the light to the back of your throat. Concentrate on that area and then relax it.

Then imagine the light traveling down into your throat. Concentrate on that area and then relax it. Then feel the light traveling down across your shoulders. Concentrate on your shoulders and then relax them. Take the light down into one of your upper arms. Repeat the process, moving the light in turn to your elbow and your hand. Then slowly bring the light back up your arm and across your shoulder toward your other arm, and repeat the process with that arm. Then bring the light slowly back up that arm and across your shoulder to your chest.

Repeat the process with your chest, your abdomen, and your groin. Then slowly take the light down into one of your thighs. Repeat the process, stopping at the knee, the lower leg, and the foot. Then imagine the light slowly traveling back up your leg and going across your groin to the other leg. Repeat the process with that leg.

Then imagine the light slowly traveling back through the trunk of your body and your throat until it reaches a point midway between your eyebrows. Keep the light there for a few moments, concentrating on that area and then relaxing it. Open your eyes.

Technique 2

Close your eyes. Going slowly down your body, mentally feel everything that touches it: the chair, the floor, your clothing.

Then feel your whole body at once. Hold that feeling for a moment. Next, imagine your body slowly being pulled down by gravity.

Note your breathing. Do not try to change it; simply experience it. Then imagine that the air you are breathing is a particular color.

On your next inhalation, imagine you are drawing your breath down with the soles of your feet, turning it around, and then sending it back with the soles of your feet. Continue doing this for several breaths. Imagine you are bringing goodness to your feet with this colored breath, bathing them, and then sending the colored breath back out, bearing away all impurities.

After a while, focus on your knees and imagine they are drawing your breath down to them, turning it around, and sending it back out.

Repeat this process with a spot just below your navel, your chest, your throat, your sinuses (just behind your nose), and the top of your head.

Then concentrate on the spot just below your nostrils. Without causing any change in your breathing, concentrate on that spot until you can feel the coldness of the air going in and the warmth of the air coming out. Remain with the awareness for several moments. Open your eyes.

Technique 3

Take your first, middle, or last name, whichever is easiest, and rearrange any or all of the letters until they form a pleasing one- or two-syllable word that is meaningless and easy to pronounce.

Close your eyes. With your lids shut, cast your eyes slightly upward, as if you were focusing on a spot between your eyebrows. Imagine you are hearing the word you created at this particular spot every time you inhale, expelling any other thought-sounds every time you exhale. Imagine your head feeling lighter and cleaner as you continue this process, until it reaches a state of optimum lightness and cleanness. Continue in this state for several moments. Open your eyes.

"To be shaken out of the ruts of ordinary perception, to be shown for a few timeless hours the outer and the inner world, not as they appear to an animal obsessed with words and notions, but as they apprehended, directly and unconditionally, by Mind at Large—this is an experience of inestimable value to everyone." —Aldous Huxley

Visualization

The major mode of perception for most human beings is visual, and our culture reflects this. We live in a visually oriented world of television and movies, computers and video games, books, magazines, newspapers, memos, reports and letters, directional signs and symbols, flowcharts, blueprints, X rays, and fashion statements. Even in the privacy of our own mind, we are inclined to think in terms of pictures, forming mental images to render complex data more intelligible or to translate information and experience into more memorable and communicable forms. Seeing is, indeed, believing.

To test how dependent you are on your powers of visualization, try this experiment. Attempt to re-create your entire day so far in terms of pictures, beginning from the moment you awoke and proceeding on through the rest of the day in chronological order. Imagine you are producing a more or less continuous film without any sound. Do not get stuck if you cannot remember a particular time period, and do not go back and insert images that you recall later. Simply go forward and note all the images that come to mind. When you have finished, start from the beginning of your day and this time think of the sounds you heard in chronological order, being careful not to refer to any visual images. Then try the same procedure with smells, tastes, tactile sensations. It is very difficult, almost impossible, to summon up sounds, smells, tastes, and tactile sensations without using visual images. Even if we are moderately successful, our list of sights is apt to be much more extensive.

To develop your awareness of hearing, smelling, tasting, and touching, you may want to experiment with the following activities:

1. Imagine giving a blind person directions for walking around your home or to a nearby store or from a public-transportation stop to your office. Do not give just kinesthetic—movement-oriented—directions (for example, how many paces the person should take before turning); also provide directions in terms of the sounds, smells, textures, and even the tastes the person may encounter.

2. The next time you are walking a familiar route, shift your consciousness from what you can see to what you can hear. During succeeding trips, choose another sensory mode and create a "map" of the impressions you receive: a smell map, a texture map, a taste map.

3. Think of the past day in terms of the following categories: hot, cold, wet, dry. Assign items you remember from the day to each category. You can do the same with hard, soft, smooth, and rough; loud, quiet, bass, and treble; and bitter, sweet, spicy, and bland.

4. From time to time, re-create mentally the sounds, smells, tastes, and textures you associate with different events, locales, time periods, or emotions.

5. Experiment with sensory-deprivation games. Take a walk (in a relatively safe environment!) with your ears plugged. Eat with your eyes closed. Watch a few moments of television with the sound off. Listen to a few moments of television with the picture completely darkened. Listen to a radio program or a record with your eyes closed. Sit near a busy street corner with your eyes closed.

Since our sense of sight, however, is our predominant mode of perception, we need to give it the most attention. The visualization techniques offered below are designed to strengthen both your conscious and your unconscious seeing abilities. The special benefits of repeated visualization training are:

• Visualization can help you give power and substance to otherwise vague ambitions. For example, by forming stronger and more personal mental pictures of what, to you, represents health or business success, you increase the chances of achieving goals in these areas.

• Visualization improves the quality of your moment-to-moment intake of visual sensations. You will learn more from what you see and remember it more easily and vividly.

• Visualization balances your tendency to think in terms of rational, linear concepts—ones that can be verbalized—by developing your ability to think in terms of images.

• Visualization provides you with a controlled and nonthreatening means of analyzing yourself and your responses to hypothetical situations.

• Visualization reveals the image content of your unconscious "storehouse." You can reclaim impressions that have been consciously forgotten but that continue to influence your thinking.

• Visualization increases your capacity to link disparate images and, therefore, to form a general picture incorporating numerous details. It further assists you in translating this general picture into an abstract idea.

Before you apply one of the techniques below, read it several times until you are confident that you can remember it. If any stray thoughts enter your mind while you are visualizing, do not fight them. Allow them to pass through your mind and gently lead your mind back to the visualization.

Technique 1

Place a small object—such as a coin, a pencil, or a shell—on a table about a foot and a half in front of a chair. Sit comfortably in the chair and look at the object for about ten seconds. Then slowly close your eyes while maintaining an overall image of the object.

After your eyes are completely closed, continue to hold this picture in your mind's eye. Do not try to project the object onto a mental screen, like the back of your eyelid, but "see" it where it is: separate from you and in front of you. Hold this sight for about fifteen seconds. Open your eyes.

In successive trials of this technique, you may want to increase gradually the complexity of the object to be visualized, proceeding, for example, to a photograph of a human face or a painting.

Technique 2

Sit comfortably in a chair turned so that you are facing most of the room in which you are sitting (or facing any scene that contains many images—a vista in a park or a view from a window). Keeping your head straight in front of you, allow your eyes to roam freely and slowly over what you see, noting not only locations and objects but also shapes, sizes, and colors. Do this for about thirty seconds to one minute. Then, staring straight ahead and attempting not to focus on anything in particular but keeping the whole scene in mind, slowly close your eyes.

While your eyes are closed, review the scene as you did while your eyes were open. Do not consider the scene as existing within your head, but imagine you are seeing it precisely where it is. Do not think about what you are seeing; simply try to see the scene as clearly and in as much detail as possible. After thirty seconds to a minute, open your eyes.

Technique 3

Assume the same posture you would for meditation, with your eyes closed. Imagine you are looking at a solid, static field of red. Hold that view for a moment.

Then imagine the color red in various natural formations, one at a time: first red clouds, then red pools, then red shadows, then red beams of light. Keep each image motionless in front of your closed eyes for several seconds. Study each image for different gradations and hues of red.

Then imagine the color red in various geometric shapes, one at a time: first a square, then a triangle, then a circle, then a sphere, then a cube. Try also imagining patterns of red, one at a time: first a checkerboard, then a plaid, then more sophisticated line and curve configurations.

Finally, imagine the color red in motion: growing from a small point to cover your entire field of vision, becoming brighter and dimmer, undulating, pulsing, spiraling, going up and down, and back and forth. Continue this for several seconds. Open your eyes.

In successive visualizations using this technique, you can substitute different colors for red.

Technique 4

Assume the same posture you would for meditation. Close your eyes. Imagine you are surrounded by an ever-thickening fog. After a while, the fog clears and you are standing in a beautiful garden on a sunny spring afternoon. It is filled with different kinds of plants and shrubs everywhere you look in front of you. Notice all the various shapes and colors of the leaves and flowers, and the play of sunlight and shadow among them.

Next, imagine you see a butterfly floating up from behind a bush. Watch it hover in front of you and then follow it with your eyes as it drifts off to your right. Turn around and continue watching it as it flies up into the blue sky, then descends and lands on the most beautiful flower of all—one you have never seen before—which grows in a small clearing protected by a low, circular hedge about a foot tall. Admire the beauty and stillness of the flower and the butterfly.

Then, keeping your eyes on the flower as the butterfly flies off, imagine you are closer and closer to the flower: more and more struck by the loveliness of its coloring, the details of its design, and its healthy vigor. Imagine it surrounded by a halo of light until all you can see is the flower and the light. Take the flower and the light into your heart. Hold this vision of peace, beauty, and life for several seconds. Open your eyes.

Technique 5

Assume the same posture you would for meditation. Close your eyes. Imagine you are standing in front of a house that you are going to enter. Take careful notice of the outside appearance of the house. What surrounds the house? What does the entrance look like?

Enter the house and wander around the rooms, making careful observations. What objects are in each room? What do the windows look like? Are they open or closed? Are there any people in the house?

Climb upstairs into the attic. What do you see? Descend into the basement. What do you see?

After a while, return to the first room you entered and sit down. Imagine you are closing your eyes and resting for several seconds. Open your eyes.

> "For me, creation starts by contemplation. . . . It is then that I work most. I look at flies, at flowers, at leaves and trees around me. I let my mind drift at ease, just like a boat in a current. Sooner or later, it is caught by something. It gets precise. It takes shape—and my next painting motif is decided."
> —Pablo Picasso

Contemplation

Contemplation is the mental discipline of relaxation and concentration that is most familiar to those of us in the Western world and so it needs the least introduction. It is the act of confining one's attention to a particular object or issue and remaining open to what that act of attention reveals.

In order to contemplate effectively, we need to disengage the part of our mind that forms value judgments, that censors impressions according to whether they are useful or not, and that urges us to categorize data step by step and arrive at practical conclusions. Bertrand Russell, the English mathematician and philosopher, once described contemplation as "pure thinking—the conscious mind activity that is distinct from, but directly precedes, idea formation."

The benefits of contemplation can be summarized as follows:

• Contemplation separates thought from stress. It helps you prove to yourself that you are continually in the process of thinking, that thinking is a natural function, and that it need not be associated with compulsion.

• Contemplation equips you with an alternative to goal-oriented thinking. When you reach a mental impasse trying to develop a solution to a particular problem or trying to recall a particular piece of information, you can switch to a contemplative mode of thinking. Your mind remains alert, and when you return to more goal-oriented thinking, you will be refreshed and more likely to achieve your goal.

• Contemplation stimulates your imagination, and therefore your creativity, by enabling you to reprocess information free from preconceived ideas and attitudes.

• Contemplation prevents you from forgetting partially complete thoughts, vague images, and nonverbalized feelings that may eventually be useful to you. It provides you with a space and framework for keeping these thoughts, images, and feelings alive.

Technique 1

Consider the blob! Find an irregularly shaped spot on a nearby wall or create an irregularly shaped spot by splashing a drop of ink or colored liquid onto a piece of paper. Then focus your eyes on the spot and think of as many different things as you can that the spot suggests or resembles.

Begin with the first things that come to your mind. If you run out of impressions, try altering your focus: Squint your eyes, change the angle at which you are viewing the spot, imagine the spot is bigger or consists of more than a single item, think of the spot as a space surrounded by its outline.

Continue for one to two minutes.

Technique 2

Assume a comfortable posture and remain still. Think of who you are, how you are, or what you are at this moment in time. Ask yourself this question: "If I were suddenly transformed into an animal, what animal would I be?" Consider what the animal would look like, as well as its environment and anything it would do or have done to it.

Repeat this activity several times, substituting "transportation vehicle," "building," "piece of furniture," "tree," "body of water," "meal," "item of clothing," "type of story," "art object," or "piece of music" for "animal."

Stick to the first image that comes to your mind each time. Spend about thirty seconds contemplating each image.

Continue applying this technique for as long as you wish.

Technique 3

Assume the same posture you would for meditation. Close your eyes. Think of several main ways you would characterize yourself at your present age. Summon visual images to represent these thoughts and formulate brief verbal descriptions of your personality, the quality of your life, your major hopes, fears, enjoyments, and trials.

Then think of yourself one year ago, using the same approach. Proceed backward year by year, spending approximately thirty seconds on each year.

Continue applying this technique for as long as you wish (or until you're born!). Then open your eyes.

In successive applications of this technique, you may want to work backward in two-, three-, four-, or five-year intervals. You may also wish to try going forward, projecting what you imagine you will be like a year from now, and so on.

Technique 4

Choose a subject—love, wisdom, farming, winter sports, your job, your neighbor. You may want to dip into a newspaper, magazine, dictionary, or nonfiction book for inspiration.

Then assume a comfortable position. Let your impressions flow freely as you mentally repeat the title of the subject every few seconds or whenever a natural pause occurs. Consider not only your own experiences and impressions but also those that are prevalent in the world around you.

Allow your mind to project simple still pictures and single-word associations as well as short moving pictures and thought fragments.

Continue this process for a couple of minutes or longer.

Any of these disciplines—meditation, visualization, or contemplation—will help you relax and concentrate. You may favor a meditation technique when you want to achieve a general state of mental clarity and flexibility, a visualization technique when you want to invoke your powers of memory and creativity, and a contemplation technique when you want to prepare your mind for rational analysis and decision-making. You may find that one discipline works best for you in all situations.

It is wise to apply at least one of the relaxation and concentration techniques, regardless of the particular discipline involved, before each mental exercise session, to create a smooth but definite break between the rest of your day and the session. It is even wiser to experiment with these techniques whenever you feel the need for a mental boost, until they become habitual means of conditioning your mind to manage more successfully the everyday stresses and strains of consciousness.

Flexibility Workouts

"Why are we wasting time with poetry in a composition course? Most of us will probably never want to read a poem, much less to write one." I had anticipated the question but not the questioner. A popular, if feisty, class member and an A student, Ruth was my neighbor's piano teacher, with twenty years' more life experience than most sophomores. "Think about learning to play the piano," I said. "Before you play songs, you practice scales—arranging and rearranging notes in patterns to make your fingers flexible and to refresh your sense of how one sound works in combination with other sounds. Studying poetry lets you do the same thing with words and images to develop your mental flexibility. That's helpful no matter what else you do."

Cultivating poetry is just one example of an activity that exercises the mind's flexibility. In countless ways, every day, voluntarily or involuntarily, we abstract ideas from the sensory images we collect or else we search for images to render ideas more palpable. It is a dynamic action and reaction process that has a counterpart in the way the body performs.

When we exercise muscles for flexibility, we are expanding them and contracting them. As we train our muscles and increase their flexibility, the operation becomes smoother, and we can feel the results. The stretch of the muscles is longer and more relaxed when we expand them, and the bulk of the muscles is greater and more solid when we contract them.

Our mind works with sensory images—the muscles it uses to produce thoughts—in much the same way. Images, like muscles, have enormous elasticity. When we expand images, we are allowing them full expression, stretching them so that they uncoil their total range of possibilities. Considering the image of a sunset, for example, you can ponder the colors, the clouds, the wind, the temperature, and the effect of the light on buildings, grass, or your skin. You can also recall any number of sunsets: the sunset on the last day of your beach vacation or the sunset while you were driving home one day last week. When we contract images, we are bending them, impressing them with meaning, and making them larger and more forceful. For example, you can forge the image of a specific sunset into a symbol of beauty, God, nature, endings, peace, drama, mystery, or romance.

A flexible mind is agile and adaptive. It tolerates ambiguity and then attempts to clarify it. It can abandon logic and habitual thought patterns and yield to free-flowing perception. And it can take charge at will, focusing on individual perceptions and impressing them with meaning.

In a 1982 nationwide survey of executive development conducted by Time Incorporated, over 80 percent of upper-level managers in *Fortune* 500 companies used the word *flexibility* when asked to describe the most important characteristic of effective thinking. A remark made by Allan Silvers, a department head for General Motors, typifies their responses. "What seems most valuable to me is a flexible mind," Silvers said. "Successful people are those who can get the big picture from details and details from the big picture."

The exercises in this chapter direct your attention back and forth between specific images and general ideas in original and thought-provoking ways. They will help you become more aware of how you think and express your thoughts more effectively to others.

Psych-up

A Walk on the Wild Side

Before they begin a psychoanalysis session, many therapists use a free-association activity to stimulate their client's mental agility. "A Walk on the Wild Side" is one of the most popular activities of this type.

To warm up before the exercises that follow, respond briefly to each image (twenty words or less, on a separate sheet of paper) with the *first* thing that comes into your mind. It does not matter if you have taken this test before, as long as you stick to your immediate reaction. Register this image clearly in your mind before you jot it down.

1. You are walking through a woods. Describe this woods.

_____

_____

2. You see a bear. Describe this bear and what happens.

_____

_____

3. You see a stranger. Describe this stranger and what happens.

_____

_____

4. You see a cup. Describe this cup and what you do with it (if anything).

_____

_____

5. You see a key. Describe this key and what you do with it (if anything).

_____

_____

6. You see water. Describe this water and what you do (if anything).

_____

_____

7. You come to a wall. Describe this wall and what you do (if anything).

_____

_____

8. Describe what is on the other side of the wall.

_____

_____

Now proceed to the next section and review your responses in light of what these images are commonly considered to symbolize.

The psych-up in this chapter stimulates your thinking about images and the ideas with which images can be linked. The symbolic interpretations offered below for each image in "A Walk on the Wild Side" are common to a wide range of psychoanalytical, literary, and artistic theories.

Individual responses you make to one of the images in "A Walk on the Wild Side" may or may not tell you about your personal psychological makeup. A response can be highly influenced by one's environment, lifestyle, and memories. "Water," for example, conjures up different images to a lifeguard, a meteorologist, or someone who lives along the Mississippi. A recent camping trip can provide an instant picture of a specific woods. Nevertheless, your responses have meaning, if only because your environment, lifestyle, and memories shape the way you think.

If you have performed "A Walk on the Wild Side" before, it will still have value—time changes one's attitudes, experiences, and mental images—but your answers will be shaded by prior knowledge of the symbolic connotations. As long as you are careful to respond with the first thing that comes into your mind (and this will become easier the more you practice it), "A Walk on the Wild Side" can be used profitably many times. You can then weave your own "walks on the wild side" as you go along, employing different images and pondering what your responses could mean.

Woods: Life in general—the "landscape" one inhabits. A dark forest choked with trees may suggest a situation that is gloomy and full of obstacles. A sunlit grove with room for small animals to scamper may reflect a more lively and optimistic life view.

Bear: Love—a large, natural phenomenon, soft and easily tamed, but potentially threatening, even overwhelming, to the psyche. Avoiding a menacing-looking bear could symbolize a self-protective attitude toward love. Making contact with a cuddly cub could represent a more easygoing approach to love.

Stranger: Friendship—one's general "social feeling" as well as the basic character of one's individual relationships with others. Interacting with the stranger may suggest an eagerness to engage with others. If the stranger is a member of the opposite sex, it may indicate that friendship with members of the opposite sex is more significant than friendship with members of the same sex.

Cup: Hope—something that can be filled or emptied, that is capable of providing nourishment. A beautiful cup may symbolize hope as something of value. Picking up the cup could mean that one possesses hope.

Key: Knowledge—a tool, something that can open doors. A car key may represent a respect for practical knowledge, as opposed to a more ornate key, which would indicate more of a respect for knowledge of the beautiful. Taking the key in hand would suggest that one feels knowledgeable.

Water: Sex—fluid, an element where one is not on one's feet, typically, or in control, one that is associated closely with life and death, pleasure and pain. A puddle may indicate small consideration for sex; a pond or a lake, larger consideration; an ocean or a river—bodies of water whose entire boundaries cannot be seen—a more "continual" concern with sex. Going into the water may symbolize a wish for sexual engagement.

Wall: Death—a stopping point. A large, imposing wall may suggest strong feelings toward death. Climbing over the wall or walking through it may symbolize that death is not viewed as an obstacle.

Other side: Afterlife—whatever is conceived to lie on the other side of death. A formal landscape or construction may represent structured beliefs about what happens after death or a desire for such beliefs. A continuation of the same landscape would indicate that one feels part of the rhythm of life that goes on even after one's own death. An entirely different type of landscape would suggest death as a different existence in a new dimension.

More Psych-ups

In future sessions, follow the same procedure outlined in the original psych-up, either with the same group of images or with any group or randomly selected images. Remember that an image is something that exists in the physical world—in other words, something that you can see, hear, touch, taste, or smell.

You can prepare for future psych-ups by writing down a lot of individual images from time to time on separate slips of paper and dropping these slips into a large box, bowl, or envelope. Then, when you begin a flexibility exercise session, you can dip into these slips and, without looking, select five for a psych-up. Simply write down the first description that comes to mind as you confront yourself with each image.

It is not necessary to interpret your responses according to a list of commonly accepted symbolic meanings, like the one used above to interpret "A Walk on the Wild Side." Just ponder each response, asking yourself why you may have reacted the way you did—what you feel the response means.

This psych-up also works well in a group. Try leading one or more friends through "A Walk on the Wild Side." Then, when all responses have been made—orally or in writing—explain the symbols in general terms and discuss possible interpretations based on specific responses. You can also take turns providing a string of spontaneous images capable of stimulating free association from the other participant(s), then discuss what the possible meanings of the resulting responses may be.

Exercise 1

What Does Freedom Look Like?: Linking the Abstract to the Concrete

The hallmark of human intelligence is the ability to make a connection between a specific sensation—something that can be seen, heard, touched, smelled, or tasted—and a general concept.

A cough is a specific sensation. You can hear it, and if it is your own cough, you can feel its texture. Your mind relates that cough to illness, which is an abstraction. In doing this, you move from the real world to the world of ideas. The process becomes so automatic to most of us by the time we are adults that we often fail to sit down and think about the meanings we give to our sensations, or about what the images are that give life to our ideas. We want success and power, but what details do we associate with these qualities? And why? Charles Schulz realized the inability of most people to define abstractions and captivated millions of Americans with his series of cartoons, *Happiness Is a Warm Puppy*.

By challenging yourself to forge links between the abstract and the concrete, you revitalize your intellectual capacities. You exercise both your ability to reach through ideas to the images that spark them and your ability to pump images for the ideas they symbolize.

List specific images that you associate with each of the following abstractions. You can either put down the first thing to pop into your head, or give it some thought. Try to complete every category of sensation; since we live in a visually oriented world, it may be easier to fill in the "sight" category than the others. Then explain briefly your response for each category.

EXAMPLE:

Freedom

sight: blue sky   *explanation:* openness, weightlessness, purity

sound: children singing   *explanation:* untrained voices, flowing unselfconsciously

touch: satin sheets   *explanation:* frivolous purchase, slide along skin *smell:* salty sea air   *explanation:* summer vacation, boundlessness of ocean

taste: coffee   *explanation:* break during work hours, rest after a meal, an indulgence I restrict

1. Love

sight: *explanation:*

sound: *explanation:*

touch: *explanation:*

smell: *explanation:*

taste: *explanation:*

2. Childhood

sight: *explanation:*

sound: *explanation:*

touch: *explanation:*

smell: _____ explanation: _____

_____

taste: _____ explanation: _____

_____

3. February

sight: _____ explanation: _____

_____

sound: _____ explanation: _____

_____

touch: _____ explanation: _____

_____

smell: _____ explanation: _____

_____

taste: _____ explanation: _____

_____

4. Achievement

sight: _____ explanation: _____

_____

sound: _____ explanation: _____

_____

touch: _____ explanation: _____

_____

smell: _____ *explanation:* _____

_____

taste: _____ *explanation:* _____

_____

More Workouts

• Use different abstract terms. Browse through books, magazines, dictionaries, and thesauruses to find such terms if none spring to mind.

• Think up several different images in each category of sensation. Begin by using the list of abstractions offered above and then move on to others.

• Jot down abstract terms that you use or encounter during the course of a day. During a later exercise session, write down the sensory images that you associate with these abstractions.

Exercise 2

Parallel Bars: Analogies

Early in this century, Ernest Rutherford's revolutionary theory about the structure of the atom excited his colleagues but failed to receive the consideration he felt it deserved in the scientific world. The breakthrough came when he proposed an analogy, suggesting that the movement of the electrons around the nucleus is similar to the orbiting of the planets around the sun. Rutherford not only made his idea more accessible, but also gained further insights into the original hypothesis.

Through practice in forming analogies, you can develop your power to detect similarities among different phenomena—a power than can broaden your understanding of new fields and enhance your ability to express that understanding.

Create a complete analogy for each of the following statements. Each lacks one or more of the elements in the analogy, and all lack a short explanation of how the analogy makes sense. Experiment with your answers. An analogy can be completed with a number of different answers, but the best answer is the one that makes the most sense to you.

EXAMPLE:

Paint is to the wall as skin is to the body.

explanation: Skin is a thin continuous layer that covers and protects the body just as paint is a thin continuous layer that covers and protects the wall. Both are also characterized by pigmentation, aging, peeling, and pores.

OR

Paint is to the wall as clothing is to the body.

explanation: Clothing covers and protects the body just as paint covers and protects the wall. Both represent decorative choices. Clothing is not essential to the structure of the body just as paint is not necessary for the wall to function architecturally.

1. _____ is to a meal as a smile is to a conversation.

explanation: _____

_____

2. A garden is to the ground as _____ is to the brain.

explanation: _____

_____

3. Water is to ice as fear is to _____ .

explanation: _____

_____

4. _____ is to the business executive as _____ is to the minis-
ter.

explanation: _____

_____

5. A map is to _____ as _____ is to time.

explanation: _____

_____

6. _____ is to a newspaper as _____ is to an orchestra.

explanation: _____

_____

7. Las Vegas is to gamblers as New York is to _____ .

explanation: _____

_____

8. _____ is to silk as rock is to marble.

explanation: _____

_____

9. A canoe is to _____ as a wagon is to _____ .

explanation: _____

_____

10. _____ is to football as _____ is to politics.

explanation: _____

_____

Malumas and Tuckatees

Which shape looks like it should be called *maluma,* and which shape looks like it should be called *tuckatee*?

a   b

Wolfgang Köhler, the Gestalt psychologist, illustrated the natural inclination of the average person to make significant metaphorical connections between random items by asking subjects to match the nonsense words *maluma* and *tuckatee* to these same two abstract figures. Without exception, his subjects related the first term to A and the second term to B.

More Workouts

• Think up a pair of words for each of the following categories:

1. two parts of a whole (for example, both a door and a window are parts of a room)

2. a whole and one of its parts (for example, a tree is part of a forest)

3. opposites or contrasts (for example, comedy and tragedy are opposites—they are diametrically different from each other; refrigerator and stove can more precisely be called contrasts—they are similar in many respects, dissimilar in others)

4. cause and effect (for example, injustice can cause anger; anger can be an effect of injustice)

  Set up each pair as the first half of an analogy (for example, "A door is to a window as . . ."). Then think of as many pairs as you can that effectively complete the analogy.

• Keep a record of the analogies you encounter in conversations or while reading or watching television programs or movies. In subsequent exercise sessions, write down all the ways in which selected analogies make sense. Try to come up with improved or related analogies.

Exercise 3

A Book Is a Sailboat: Metaphors

"My home is a circus, a battlefield, a haven in a storm." When I offer such comparisons, I am speaking in metaphors. A metaphor is a riddle that is easily solved by flexing the mind. "My home is a circus" associates my home with an image of frenzy and spectacle; it captures and communicates how I perceive my home at a given moment.

A metaphor may be thought of as a compressed analogy. When we say a familiar face is to a crowd as an oasis is to a desert, we are saying a familiar face is an oasis, or a crowd is a desert. A good metaphor delights the imagination and inspires the rational mind to forge new truths.

Consider what each of the following words means to you. Ask yourself, "What sensations does the word conjure up? What do I associate with the word? With what things can the word be compared?" Then find a concrete image that works as a metaphor for the word. Finally, tell why the metaphor makes sense.

EXAMPLE:

A book is a sailboat.

explanation: It is designed by a craftsperson to carry me to new places; I use my own skills, but

I am also carried along; I get pleasure out of the experience; I am in a different element.

1. My favorite coat is _____

explanation: _____

_____

2. My lover is _____

explanation: _____

_____

3. A skyscraper is _____

explanation: _____

_____

4. My hair is _____

explanation: _____

_____

5. A cloud is _____

explanation: _____

_____

6. A movie theater is _____

explanation: _____

_____

7. A letter is _____

explanation: _____

_____

More Workouts

• Use other concrete images that you think up or select at random from a magazine, a newspaper, or a book.

• Concentrate on one or two images and develop as many different metaphors for them as you can, explaining the sense of each metaphor you create. You can begin by using the images in the exercise above and then move on to ones you think up or select at random.

• Jot down metaphors you encounter in conversations or while reading or watching television programs or movies. In subsequent exercise sessions, write down all the ways in which the selected metaphors make sense. Create improved or related metaphors.

Figuratively Speaking

We are all in the gutter, but some of us are looking at the stars.

—Oscar Wilde

Time is but the stream I go a-fishing in.

—Henry David Thoreau

To see a world in a grain of sand
And heaven in a wild flower,
To hold Infinity in the palm of your hand,
And Eternity in an hour.

—William Blake

As crude a weapon as the cave man's club, the chemical barrage has been leveled against the fabric of life.

—Rachel Carson

Some men rob you with a six-gun—others rob you with a fountain pen.

—Woody Guthrie

I like to take well-known phrases and twist them a little. I call these phrases "mental hotfoots." Why, for instance, are there small craft warnings but no large craft warnings? If you have a heart-to-heart talk, can you have an elbow-to-elbow talk?

—George Carlin

Canada Dry tastes like love.

—ginger ale commercial

Exercise 4

The Seven Dwarfs: Discovering the Characters Within You

Snow White passed the time between living with her father and stepmother and living with her husband the prince in the company of seven dwarfs, whom Walt Disney named Happy, Grumpy, Doc, Sneezy, Sleepy, Bashful, and Dopey. A psychologist might interpret these dwarfs as representations of various aspects of Snow White's identity.

Each of us shows many faces to the world. We combine different aspects of our personality to respond to different people we meet, different roles we fill, different challenges and opportunities we encounter, and different hopes and fears we develop. Recognizing the separate characters you embody can help you cope more effectively with specific life situations as well as appreciate more fully the general patterns that influence your attitudes and behavior. To achieve this flexibility of awareness, you need to be able to cross the boundary of rational thought and think imaginatively: Who are the several people contained in the one person me?

Create at least three characters that symbolize parts of your own identity. Give each character a name. You don't have to use a common adjective as a name—a name like Chesterfield may have connotations that fit one of your characters. Your characters do not need to be dwarfs unless you feel this is appropriate for one or more of them. Briefly describe each character's body, clothing, and home, and give each character a distinctive activity and a cherished object.

EXAMPLE:

Mike is a 5′ 8″ realtor who is a husband, a father of four children, an avid racquetball player, and a dog lover. Any one of these attributes can form the basis of a character, but here is one response Mike made when he performed this exercise that I didn't anticipate:

name:	Magneto
body:	a 6′ 4″ frame topped by a shiny black pompadour
clothing:	a black silk shirt, white deck pants, lots of gold chains, and Beatle boots
home:	a penthouse with a large circular dimly lit living room lined with mirrors
distinctive activity:	meaningful eyebrow movements
cherished object:	a silver rosin dispenser with magic dancing dust

1. *name*: _____

   body: _____

   clothing: _____

   _____

   home: _____

   _____

   distinctive activity: _____

   cherished object: _____

2. *name*: _____

   body: _____

   clothing: _____

   _____

   home: _____

   _____

   distinctive activity: _____

   cherished object: _____

3. *name*: _____

   body: _____

   clothing: _____

   _____

   home: _____

   _____

   distinctive activity: _____

   cherished object: _____

More Workouts

• Create additional characters that symbolize parts of your identity. Experiment with characters that result from deeper self-examination as well as with characters that reflect your behavior or state of mind at a particular time.

• Consider people you know when you have a good opportunity to observe. Create a character for each person, just as you created several characters for yourself. Describe the character's favorite clothing, secret home, distinctive activity, and cherished object.

If you feel you know the person pretty well, go on to create other characters you feel are suggested by that person's lifestyle or personality. If you don't know the person that well, it is more difficult to create more than one character, but try it anyway. You will be articulating the impressions that you are, in fact, forming, whether you are aware of them yet or not.

• Think of a story, television show, or movie that you especially enjoy. Try recasting the roles with people you know personally or with celebrities. Briefly explain the logic behind each casting decision.

Exercise 5

Night Watch: Reclaiming Your Dreams

Dreams are like a second life. Every night while our bodies sleep, our minds invent fresh, intuitive, nonrational experiences, reinterpreting data from our daytime existence with complete freedom. Dreams can alert us to feelings, connections, and possibilities that we have failed to register consciously but that nevertheless have impressed themselves on our minds.

All of us dream every night. In fact, we usually have several periods of dreaming during a few hours of sleep. But not all of us remember our dreams. Even when we do, the memory fades quickly as logic reasserts itself and rejects confusing dream images. With effort we can not only learn to master and retain the language of dreams, adding a whole new dimension of wisdom to our lives, but also inspire cooperation between the conscious mind and the unconscious mind that can greatly enhance our mental fitness.

There are several techniques you can use to improve your ability to recall dreams. The most potent one is simply to tell yourself several times during the day that you intend to remember your dreams, and repeat this intention especially strongly just before you fall asleep. Keep a pencil and paper close to your bed. Write your dreams down, using the present tense, the moment you awake—even if it is the middle of the night. Other things you can do are:

1. Drink a glass of water before retiring. It will help you wake up faster—or more often.

2. Write down your last thoughts before retiring. This will clear your mind and may even influence the content of your dreams.

3. Set your alarm for an earlier time than usual. You may surprise yourself in the middle of a dream.

4. Lie still for a moment after awakening and concentrate on recalling your dreams.

5. Place an object with a scent—a bag of herbs, a sachet, a room deodorant—near your bed to "inspire" your dreams. The fact that you have consciously associated the scent with dreaming may trigger recall of a dream during the fuzzy moments of waking up.

Once you recall a dream, you can write it down and do the following exercise.

Identify the major images in your dream, the ones that impressed you most deeply. Consider each item as an independent term and ask yourself, "What sensation does the image conjure up? What do I associate with the image? To what other images can it be compared?" Then relate your answers to anything that you experienced the day before, paying special attention to your last waking thoughts. Finally, record briefly what you feel the dream is discussing.

EXAMPLE:

Judy, a thirty-six-year-old designer, had this dream: "I have broken into an empty apartment. I have the feeling I have just rented this apartment, or I am going to rent it. It is absolutely bare and dusty. The walls are gray-white. I open a closet and find a red dress. It is daring and loud and not the type of dress I'd buy for myself. It is my old size—6—and seems brand new, even though the style is quaint. I try it on and it fits well. I see myself in a dark mirror and I like how I look."

major images:	empty apartment, red dress
associations:	empty apartment—looked like the apartment I had in college, poor-person's apartment, lifeless, but big and mysterious red dress—red is a passionate color; the dress seemed a bit like a costume; I felt it was a bonus, an unexpected gift I got with the apartment
day before:	met an old friend from college who might know of a new job for me; the day was overcast; I worried about aging; before falling asleep I wondered about whether I would get the job
discussion:	the dream seems to be about my possible new job—starting over, like in college; even though I have my doubts and fears (the images of big, mysterious, dark), I have a passion for it—I want it and somehow I feel it suits me, will give me a new identity that I will like

major images: _____

_____

associations: _____

_____

_____

_____

day before: _____

_____

_____

_____

discussion: _____

_____

_____

_____

Dreams Come True

Einstein traces his relativity theory to a dream he had when he was an adolescent. He was riding on a sled, and as he went faster and faster, the stars became distorted.

Mendeleyev developed the structure of the Periodic Table of Elements after dreaming of a concert of chamber music.

Mary Shelley based *Frankenstein* on a dream she had about Lord Byron, who at the time was creating a poem, "Manfred," about a character that closely resembled himself.

Elias Howe was inspired to create a new design for the sewing-machine needle after dreaming he was in a cauldron, surrounded by cannibals who kept thrusting spears at him.

Kekule von Stradonitz dreamed of a twisting snake biting its tail and awoke with the molecular structure of the benzene ring.

Niels Bohr derived the quantum theory from a dream of a racetrack.

Robert Louis Stevenson dreamed the plot of *Dr. Jekyll and Mr. Hyde,* in which the doctor character saw a picture of a jackal just before his transformation.

Descartes went in and out of sleep to dream parts of his *Discourse on Reason.*

Eleanor Roosevelt thought sentences in a dream that she later managed to incorporate in the United Nations charter.

Dante claimed he received both the form and much of the content of *The Divine Comedy* from a series of dreams he had while traveling.

Coleridge transcribed his unfinished poem "Kubla Khan" directly from a dream he had that was interrupted by the arrival of an insurance salesman.

More Workouts

• Dreams are often associated with movies. They appear to be a special form of entertainment provided for us while we are a captive audience. Take a recent dream and imagine that it is a movie. Pick a title that would look good on a marquee—one that not only fits your dream but that is intriguing. Then give a brief summary of the dream-movie, like the ones that appear in newspaper film reviews, or TV magazines.

• Imagine your dream is a real-life event that is being reported in a newspaper or magazine. Give it an appropriate headline and a one-paragraph report. Try out different styles: Imagine the article is appearing in *The New York Times,* the *National Enquirer, Reader's Digest,* or *Psychology Today*.

• Write a continuation of a recent dream. What happens after the point at which the dream stops? You can also experiment with filling in the missing parts of the dream: scene shifts that seem to be missing or conversations you do not quite remember.

• If your dream has more than one character, practice shifting points of view. Imagine you are perceiving the dream from the point of view of each of the characters appearing in the dream, one by one. Describe each dream picture that results.

Mind Play

1. Identify images that you feel represent your personality, interests, way of life, background, and values. Then use these images to create a personal flag, monogram, coat of arms, or stamp.

2. Imagine that you are filling a time capsule to be opened a thousand years from now. You cannot include any books or magazines or texts that explain the contents. You need to include items that appeal to all five senses (individual items need appeal to only one sense or any combination of senses). What would you place in a time capsule specifically designed to represent the 1960s? The 1970s? The 1980s? Your own life as a whole? The life of someone you know well?

3. Think of people you know and ask yourself, for each one, "What animal does this person resemble?" The resemblance need not be physical—it may be a resemblance in behavior or style.

4. Try incubating a dream. Before you go to sleep, concentrate on what you want to dream about or what you want your dream to be like. You may want to write out a dream like the one you wish to have just before retiring, then compare that written dream with the one you do have. Successfully incubating a dream takes practice, so don't be discouraged if there are no discernible results right away.

More Flexibility Exercises

• The three cardinal virtues are faith, hope, and charity; the seven deadly sins are pride, sloth, gluttony, lust, envy, greed, and anger. Cub Scouts must be trustworthy, honest, loyal, brave, kind, clean, and reverent.

Take one of these abstractions—or any other abstraction you encounter—and relate it to specific images. How would you depict the abstraction to a child, your peers, a visitor from outer space? Try to use images that relate to each of the senses.

• Compare your own experience to that of others—the people you know, the people you read about, and the people you observe. How is your life like that of an astronaut? What in your own experience is like your neighbor's enthusiasm for sports cars? Why?

• Look through a magazine or a book with lots of pictures. Make lists of the images that strike you. Then create metaphors for those images.

Record images on file cards—one image to a card. Then choose any two cards at random and attempt to make sense of the "forced" metaphor. For example, two cards may say *toaster* and *house cat*. Some thinking can result in the following explanation: "A house cat is a toaster. The love you put into it can suddenly pop out and nourish you."

• College poetry textbooks contain explanations and examples of figures of speech—not only symbols, analogies, and metaphors but also personifications, metonymies, synecdoches, similes, and many others. Even better, they provide exercises for you to develop your understanding and appreciation of figurative language.

Choose a text you like and give the exercises to yourself. Frequently, the publisher will be able to send you a teacher's edition upon request that contains further information as well as answer keys to the exercises.

• Bruno Bettelheim, an internationally renowned child psychologist, describes the symbolic value of classic fairy and folk tales to a child's mental and emotional development in his book *The Uses of Enchantment*. Consider the stories that you enjoyed most or that your children enjoy. Examine each story as you would a dream. Which images seem to be symbols? Why do they have special meaning to you?

• Keep a dream journal in which you record your dreams each night. After a few dreams, note any recurring or analogous images. Count the times different types of images appear in your dreams—for instance, threatening strangers, green objects, doorways. Ask yourself, "Why these images now?"

• An allegory is a system of symbols that can work together to create a story. Throughout human history, people have devised allegorical systems to attempt to make sense of things that lie beyond the capacity of rational understanding. Among the most widely used allegorical systems are astrology, tarot, the I-ching, runes, and the medicine wheel. Such systems are of value regardless of whether they reveal any truths in a realistic sense because working with them frees the mind from the restraints of logic. If particular symbols do have meaning for the person who considers them, it is perhaps because pondering what they represent has liberated his or her imagination and has allowed new associations to reveal themselves. The fact that the allegorical systems mentioned above have survived for centuries and continue to be meaningful in countless lives can be attributed to their value as imaginative resources worth studying.

Familiarize yourself with the five allegorical systems mentioned above and choose one for your own exercise in mental flexibility. Each can provide you with a new set of images—images you can manipulate to form metaphors, symbols, and analogies.

• Keep alert while you are listening to yourself as well as to other people for spoken metaphors. Can you observe any patterns? Does the same type of metaphor reappear regularly to describe a certain phenomenon? Do you or does someone else use a certain kind of metaphor again and again to describe different phenomena? What possible meaning might this have?

Memory Workouts

Gort! Klaatu barada nikto.

I once encountered these words spray-painted on a Wall Street building. They were hauntingly familiar, but after wracking my brain again and again, I still could not identify them. A couple of weeks later, I was watching a movie on television that I had loved as a child, *The Day the Earth Stood Still,* and suddenly I heard the visitor from another planet speak these words to the Earthwoman, Patricia Neal. They were a secret command for gaining access to his spaceship, and for the rest of the movie she struggled to retain the odd-sounding phrase in her memory. Recently I saw this movie again, and even though I knew in advance that the magic words were *Gort! Klaatu barada nikto,* I could still agonize with Patricia Neal's efforts to remember such a critical piece of information.

All knowledge is based on memory—the interplay of recognition and recall. It is therefore particularly distressing when we are unable to attach a name to the face of a person to whom we have been introduced before or when we forget where we put an important document or when we cannot reconstruct the meaning of a note we made to ourselves some months back that says something like "spiral . . . friendship . . . Ohio." Somehow, our entire store of facts, ideas, and impressions seems threatened, and we lose sense of how much data we actually do hold in our mind and how inexhaustible our capacity for memory is.

The ability to remember something rests on three different principles: repetition, interest, and association. We can passively allow one or more of them to function as it will, or we can actively engage one or more of them to ensure that our memory works for us as effectively as we want it to work.

There is almost no limit to how much we can remember if we set our minds to it. Famous examples of the results of self-imposed memory training abound. During six weeks of part-time effort, the American philosopher William James taught himself to recite all twelve books of John Milton's *Paradise Lost* without error, just to prove to himself that he could do it. Charles W. Eliot, president of Harvard University for forty years, once suffered such acute embarrassment because he forgot a student's name that he became determined to improve his memory. He studied all the techniques he could find, and for the rest of his years at Harvard he could name each undergraduate student simply by looking at a photograph. Because he knew it would ultimately make life easier, Arturo Toscanini acquired the ability to conduct symphonies without the assistance of written scores.

Your ambitions may not be so grandiose. But whatever they are, exercising your memory can bolster your pride, save you from potentially embarrassing moments, and make daily life less complicated.

If we consciously return to a particular fact or impression again and again, we create a new thought habit, one that stands a good chance of being easily triggered in the future. Memorizing by repetition requires concentration: putting ourselves through drills and reapplying these drills at different periods of time. Such a process is by itself a mental-discipline program that can improve one's willpower and self-respect. But repetition is essentially unexciting and does not immediately invite commitment.

The more we are interested in something, the easier it is to remember and the more inspired we are to commit ourselves to the task of remembering. Our interest may arise automatically from the subject, according to our individual predisposition. For example, a sports enthusiast not interested in politics will find it much easier to master football lore than the history of the Republican Party.

We can also deliberately decide to take an interest in something different by gearing ourselves mentally to remain open-minded and to accept the importance of the fact we are confronting or the person we are meeting. Enforcing our attention can be a game we play or a serious venture. Either way, we are more apt to increase our memory potential.

Many people have a preestablished incentive to memorize—to help themselves succeed in a specific test situation. If you do not have a built-in reason, you can give yourself one by repeating to yourself briefly the purpose of memorizing something before you begin to do so. That purpose can be as general as "gaining material for contemplation or conversation," "doing better in my work," or simply, "building my memory skills." The more specific your goal is, however, the more motivated you will be to memorize.

By far the most effective memory aid is associating the item to be remembered with something else. The human brain has a natural tendency to do this anyway in ways that are whimsical, logical, and psychological. William James wrote: "The secret of a good memory is the secret of forming diverse and multiple associations with every fact we care to retain." You may recall a passage in a novel you once read by thinking of the park where you read it. You may find that envisioning a highway pattern helps you remember the design of the body's circulatory system. Or you may be able to recollect the name of a store you once patronized by reviewing other events that occurred on the last day you visited it or the person who waited on you or the logo on the receipt.

Mnemonics are memory-enhancing tricks that link unfamiliar or confusing data with something that can be quickly recalled. Among these mnemonics are acronyms (memory words made up of the first letters of a list of items, such as "Roy G. Biv" for the colors in a rainbow); acrostics (memory sentences, in which each word begins with a letter that corresponds to a specific item in a list, such as "Do musicians ever visit Boston?" for the British ranks of peerage—duke, marquis, earl, viscount, and baron); and infectious catch phrases containing rhymes or particularly vivid images (such as "Thirty days hath September, April, June, and November" for month lengths, and "spring forward, fall back" for how to adjust a clock to daylight savings time).

The exercises in this chapter will show you numerous ways to use repetition, interest, and association to imprint new information successfully and to stimulate recall.

Acronyms

BOPEEP: Bangor Orange Position Estimating Equipment for Pastures—an electronic beeper attached to sheep by herders in Bangor, Wales

BUSSTOP: Breathers United to Stop Standing Time Of Passenger-buses—a student legal action group

CREEP: Committee for the REElection of the President—organization of Nixon supporters during the 1972 U.S. presidential campaign.

EGADS: Electronic Ground Automatic Destruct System—signal given to intercept an in-flight missile

GASP: Group Against Smog and Pollution

GIMPY: Growing, Improving, Maturing Puppy of the Year—a canine award

HOMES: Huron, Ontario, Michigan, Erie, and Superior—the Great Lakes

IRAC: Issue, Rule, Application, and Conclusion—stages of law history

POCO: Physiology Of Chimpanzees in Orbit—a NASA (National Aeronautics and Space Administration) term

SANE: Safe Alternatives to Nuclear Energy—a citizens' action group

VIOLENT: Viewers Intent On Listing violent Episodes on Nationwide Television—a student legal action group

Acrostics

All **C**ows **E**at **G**rass: the notes that fall in the spaces of a musical staff, bass clef

Good **B**oys **D**o **F**ine: the notes that fall on the lines of a musical staff, bass clef

Kings **P**lay **C**hess **O**n **F**ine-**G**rained **S**and: the biological categories, proceeding from the most general (**K**ingdom, **P**hylum, **C**lass, **O**rder, **F**amily, **G**enus, **S**pecies)

My **V**ery **E**conomical **M**other **J**ust **S**aved **U**s **N**ine **P**ercent: the order of the planets, starting from the sun (Mercury, Venus, Earth, Mars, Jupiter, Saturn, Uranus, Neptune, Pluto).

Put **E**ggs **O**n **M**y **P**late, **P**lease: the different geologic epochs, in chronological order (Paleocene, Eocene, Oligocene, Miocene, Pliocene, Pleistocene)

Six **C**ampers **P**acked **H**eavily: the four varieties of schizophrenia (simple, catatonic, paranoid, and hebephrenic)

Psych-up

Pass It Along

Young children are fairly quick to recognize something they have seen, touched, heard, smelled, or experienced before; but when they are actually directed to recall something specific, such as what they did yesterday morning, their performance is likely to be very poor. They are not yet aware that there are techniques for remembering things. Formal education is built on memory training. It instills in us the desire to remember. It also introduces us to a range of external memory systems, like notes, outlines, and reference books. Being able to rely on external memory systems is, however, a mixed blessing. Frequently, I find myself not bothering to generate thought about a project or a problem because I do not have access to pencil and paper to jot down ideas or to books that would provide additional information or would induce further thought. Many times I have forgotten shopping lists and cannot recall what I wanted because I didn't bother committing the items to memory. Too often we do not concentrate on remembering what we are reading because we know we have a permanent record.

Try this experiment. Do not look back at the preceding paragraph. Write down on a sheet of paper what it said, as if you were passing it along to someone else. Do not spend more than two or three minutes writing down what you remember, and try to avoid rereading and rewriting.

When you have finished, compare your version to the original paragraph. Then read the following discussion.

Whenever you want to remember something that you are reading or hearing, it helps to keep track of groups of key words and phrases as they occur. In the passage you were just asked to recall, such groups of key words and phrases could be:

> children . . . recognize
> directed to recall . . . performance . . . poor
> formal education . . . memory training
> external memory systems . . . notes
> external memory systems . . . mixed blessing
> not bothering . . . cannot recall . . . do not concentrate

Each of these groups cues us to recall a main point in the original paragraph.

Check your own version of the paragraph and see if you missed any of these main points. Even more important, check to see if you distorted the meaning of the original points, however slightly, in your version. For example, one person who did this experiment wrote, "Children remember things they have touched or seen before; but when you ask them directly about it, they do very poorly." In the original paragraph, a distinction is made between "recognizing" and "recalling" that is not made in the subject's version. Reading the latter, one is apt to think that the author is accusing children of being intimidated by or resistant to questioning. Perhaps this is an idea that is more familiar to the subject and so she unconsciously substituted it for the author's idea, which has somewhat similar wording.

Often, our memory of a spoken or written message is distorted by our own preconceptions or by our natural inclination to change details of individual statements so that the overall message will be easier to remember. We are also liable to remember the beginning and ending of long passages much more accurately than the middle. Making a habit of what many memory experts call rhythmic attention—latching on to a specific word or phrase every few seconds—can help you overcome these tendencies. Thinking speed works much faster than reading speed and listening speed, and consequently, our mind inevitably wanders to some degree while we are reading or listening. You can harness the extra energy of your thinking speed and use it to improve your memory in many ways:

1. From time to time during a single reading or listening experience, mentally monitor whether or not you are retaining what you are reading or hearing in the exact form in which it is being presented.

2. Identify and suspend any prejudices or preconceptions you may have about what you are hearing or reading.

3. Make a mental record of the physical details in your reading or listening environment. If you are reading a book, for example, periodically take note of the type, the quality of light, your posture, nearby objects. If you are listening to someone speaking in front of you, check out that person's gestures, mannerisms, and clothing. Ask yourself, "What messages am I receiving from this person's body language? How do they relate to what I am hearing?"

4. Formulate and keep track of any questions you have about what you are reading or hearing. If you are reading, you can go back over the material when you have finished, seeking answers to the questions, or you can investigate other sources. In a face-to-face listening situation, you can check out the answers to your questions by posing them directly to the speaker or by conducting your own research later.

5. Imagine you are reading what you are hearing or hearing what you are reading. Doing the former may help you to take the information more seriously. You will minimize visual distractions and come closer to hearing what is being said as if it were spoken inside your own head. Hearing what you are reading also creates what can be called a stereophonic effect: You subconsciously register images more precisely and make yourself more aware of the sound potential of the mute words before you.

More Psych-ups

In future exercise sessions, follow the same procedure outlined in the original psych-up with any block chosen at random from a newspaper, magazine, or book. Read the block only once before you begin. Experiment with different types of texts, including fiction and nonfiction. Choose blocks of text that are at least two hundred words long (this is about half of a standard 8½" by 11" printed page). As you become more adept, you can use longer passages. This activity is doubly beneficial if you select material you want to remember for some reason apart from simply performing a psych-up.

"A memory is a piece of mindmusic—a face a name a fact a thing when we first perceive it that becomes a beat a tone a pitch a chord in our mind-score"—Jack Kerouac

Exercise 1

Past Perfect: Guided Recall

At least once in your life you have probably had the mildly frightening experience of completing a familiar route and then drawing a blank when you tried to remember passing major landmarks along the way. Your brain had brought you safely to your destination, but you remained unconscious of what was happening.

You may have marveled at the mind's ability to do this. You may have given thanks to God or nature. But you probably also felt a sense of loss, as if you had missed several moments of life. Unfortunately, moments of unlived life are not confined to this particular type of experience.

By making a conscious effort to focus on what occurs to you each moment, you greatly increase the chance that you will remember it—and remember it easily—in the future. Then, when moments come along that you purposely want to remember, you will be all the more successful in doing so, thanks to your sustained practice in concentrating.

You can monitor how effectively you focus on what occurs to you by periodically reexamining past events to determine how particular and how various are the details you can recall. You will find that your whole past becomes more alive the more you do this because as you build a clearer and more elaborate reconstruction of a single event, you will stimulate associations with other events as well.

Recall each of the following events. Try to form a vivid mental image of each event. Then answer the questions with as much detail as you can.

EXAMPLE:

The last time you visited a doctor's office:
What different noises did you hear?

- the wheezing and banging of an old elevator: a scary sound

- a man speaking with a West Indian accent in the chair next to me—talking about Dagwood sandwiches

- the "pump . . . pump" sound of a blood-pressure bulb

What different colors did you observe?

- the pale green and dirty yellow office carpeting

- the receptionist's shiny gold blouse

- the red-striped bandage wrapper

- the clear, especially deep blue sky outside the office window

1. The most recent evening you spent with a relative:

What did that relative say?

_____

_____

What clothes did that relative wear?

_____

_____

2. Four days ago:

What did you eat?

_____

_____

What is the last thing you did before you went to sleep?

_____

_____

How did you feel physically?

_____

_____

3. The last time you smelled a very strong, distinctive odor:

What did the environment look like?

_____

_____

What happened next?

_____

_____

4. Your most recent birthday:

What was the weather like?

_____

_____

What presents and other acknowledgments did you receive?

_____

_____

5. A time when you did something forbidden:

What were you wearing?

_____

_____

What time of day was it?

_____

_____

What thoughts did you have before, during, and after?

_____

_____

"Aristotle could have avoided the mistake of thinking that women have fewer teeth than men by the simple device of asking Mrs. Aristotle to open her mouth."—Bertrand Russell

6. The first hour you were awake this morning:

What different noises did you hear?

_____

_____

What different emotional feelings did you have?

_____

_____

How Much Do We Remember?

According to information theory, a *bit* is the smallest unit of information: equal to a simple yes or no. Mathematician John Griffith claims that the lifetime capacity of the average human memory is 10^{11} (one hundred trillion, or 100,000,000,000,000) bits. John von Neumann, an information theorist, sets the figure at 2.8×10^{20} (280 quintillion, or 280,000,000,000,000,000,000) bits. The von Neumann total, unlike the Griffith total, assumes that nothing is ever forgotten; but even if we assume that only one tenth of 1 percent of whatever we learn in life is retained—an amount much lower than the most conservative scientific estimate—it would still mean that our memory contains several billion times more information than the most sophisticated computer yet devised.

More Workouts

• Where appropriate, transpose the questions listed under one event to another event. Include the event and the questions posed in the introductory example.

• Select a month—for example, April. Beginning with the past year, go back year by year and recall as many specific sensory images as you can that reflect what occurred that month. You can perform the same activity using holidays or recurrent milestones in your personal or working life.

• Here is a list of some common experiences. Choose one or more items for a single exercise session and recall as many specific sensory images that relate to that event as you can:

>You threw away something you did not want.

>You got back something you had lost.

>You were correct to disobey.

>You got away with something.

>You did something you did not want to do and enjoyed yourself.

>You felt honored.

>You narrowly escaped disaster.

>You were struck by the beauty of someone.

>You decided to overlook something.

>You got what you deserved.

>You were shocked.

>You won an argument.

Exercise 2

Everything in Its Place: Remembering Sequence

Twenty-four hundred years ago, Simonides, a Greek rhetorician, was attending a banquet on the island of Ceos when an earthquake struck. He survived unscathed, but many of the guests reclining at the table were crushed beneath heavy stones and mutilated beyond recognition. Simonides was the only one who could identify the bodies because he happened to remember which couch each person had been occupying.

Impressed by this occurrence, Simonides invented a technique that orators have used for centuries to memorize long speeches. First the speaker relates the main topics of a speech to images. Then the speaker mentally locates each image in a succession of specific places in a familiar room. Later the speaker can remember the items to cover by taking a mental walk around the room and revisualizing each image in turn. The same technique can be applied to any list of items you wish to fix in your memory.

Choose a room in which you spend a lot of time. It may be the room you inhabit now or any room you can easily visualize. Select spots around the room that are prominent and unlikely to change soon. Then imagine you see each item in the following list in a different one of these spots, going around the room in order. Take two to three minutes. At least ten minutes later, try to recall the list by mentally visualizing the room.

EXAMPLE:

You are thinking of a living room that has a beautiful bay window. To the right of the window is a plant mounted on the wall. To the right of the plant is an umbrella stand. Given three items—a pencil, yesterday afternoon, and a rubber duck—you may imagine an unsharpened yellow pencil sitting in the sun on the sill of the bay window, perhaps reflected in the glass. Moving to the next spot, you may see the words *yesterday afternoon* engraved on the wall plant holder. In the following spot you may visualize a Donald Duck bath toy, wet and glistening from a dripping umbrella.

1. a seashell
2. a lunch
3. a rope
4. a bowling ball
5. a deck of cards
6. a parking place
7. a confrontation
8. a fence
9. a puddle of water
10. a saxophone

More Workouts

• Perform the previous exercise with any list of items you want to remember.

• Read a block of printed text at least two hundred words long. Underline key words that would help you recall what you have read. Then follow the same procedure. See if it helps you to reconstruct the entire passage.

• Select different rooms occasionally when you practice this exercise. Continue to pick rooms with which you are familiar—rooms that you can visualize easily.

• Try this same technique using a familiar route. Choose places along the route to associate with different images: You can do this either by actually taking the route and visualizing the images as you come to particular landmarks or by mentally re-creating the route and picturing images at these landmarks.

Exercise 3

Apples and Elbows: Organizing Data for Better Retention

Suppose you are leaving home for the day and there are a number of items you want to remember. Although you could write them all down, you decide to trust—and exercise—your memory. You need to buy spaghetti, orange juice, milk, hamburger, lettuce, cucumbers, a box of nails, and a paintbrush. You want to talk with George about vacation plans and to Jean about her career ideas. You also plan to stop by Milton Drane's office or the library for some insurance information and to be on the lookout for a good anniversary present.

You can keep repeating these items over and over until you feel confident that you will not forget anything. A much faster and more effective method, however, is first to organize the items into categories. With this list, as with most lists, you have a number of options. You can distinguish between items that are concrete objects—the groceries, the nails, and the paintbrush—and items that are abstractions—the vacation plans, the career ideas, the insurance information, and the anniversary. You can sort the items in sequence according to an itinerary: first the supermarket (for the food and drink items), then the hardware store (for the nails and the paintbrush), then the gift shop (for the present), then the library and, finally, Jean's house. You may realize that you can make phone calls to acquire the insurance information and to speak with Jean, so you can divide your list into "visits" and "calls."

Breaking down any list—either a list of key words or a daily "to do" list—translates it into manageable sections with their own added memory triggers and increases the likelihood that you will not omit any item.

Group the items below into as many different categories as you can. Then determine at least one way in which you can organize the entire list into categories. Be imaginative, and don't be concerned about the precise meaning of each word. It is only necessary that the word itself be retained.

EXAMPLE:

account	popcorn
marry	slip
crash	raincoat
interest	boredom
whistle	nakedness

Categories: *Policewoman's clothing:* whistle, raincoat, slip
Opposites: interest/boredom, nakedness/raincoat
Sounds: whistle, popcorn, crash
Verbs: account, marry, crash, interest, whistle, slip
Nouns: raincoat, boredom, nakedness, popcorn
Banking terms: account, interest, slip
Cause and effect: slip/crash, interest/marry

*Organized
list:*   *Opposites:* interest/boredom, nakedness/raincoat
Sounds: whistle, popcorn, crash
Activities: marry, account, slip

tree   fear
warmth   sled
airplane   potato
shoe leather   steel
horse   sleep
glass

Categories:

_____

_____

_____

_____

_____

_____

_____

Organized list:

_____

_____

_____

_____

_____

_____

_____

More Workouts

• Take any body of information—a business report, what you know about the Olympics, a list of conversational topics—and spend a few moments putting items of that information into as many categories as you can. You will not only improve your recall of details, you will also increase your understanding of the information.

• Write down all the things you want to accomplish tomorrow. Reduce each item to a single word. Then do the above exercise on the list.

Exercise 4

What's in a Name?: Remembering Tough Words

If you were given the following list to memorize—wheat, division, furnace, guilt, soapsud, century—you would do much better recalling wheat, furnace, and soapsud than you would recalling division, guilt, and century. We retain words that refer to specific images more readily than words that represent abstractions.

Names of people, places, or unfamiliar concepts and objects can be even more difficult to master. Occasionally we run across a Daisy Brown or a Robin Justice, but most people have names that have no counterparts in common language—Henry Kissinger, Joe Namath, Pia Zadora. Places often bear names deliberately chosen to be distinctive—Aberdeen, Baton Rouge, the Mekong Delta. And specialized areas of knowledge often contain terms that exist in no other context—osteomyelitis, kabbalah, carburetor.

When you are introduced to someone for the first time, you can increase your chances of remembering the name by immediately repeating it aloud. Later, you can go over the name in your mind. You can apply the same technique to new place names and terms. This process is speeded up considerably, however, if you mentally alter the word, substituting another word, or group of words, that sounds similar and creates a more tangible image. The Mexican volcano Popocatepetl (pronounced poe-poe-*cawt*-ah-pet-el) can be remembered as "poppa-caught-a-petal."

The closer the substituted sounds come to the actual sound of the word, the better; but approximate sounds, or phrases that do not necessarily form a logical sentence (such as "pope, a cot, a pedal" for Popocatepetl) or words that only replicate part of the complete term (such as "pop, catapult" for Popocatepetl) are also very effective memory catalysts.

The important thing is that you turn a name or a term that is meaningless by itself into sounds that evoke tangible images. By making a habit of substituting phonetically similar words for the name or the word you want to remember, you increase your concentration on it. You also involve it with the information you already possess. By giving it these kinds of associative links, you greatly enhance the odds that you will be able to retrieve it from your memory at any time.

For each name or word, provide a more familiar substitute word or group of words that creates a similar sound. If you are uncertain about the pronunciation of a word, assign any pronunciation you wish before coming up with any substitutions.

EXAMPLE:

Holzaepfel—holds apple
Ferguson—fur goes on
Starimilceo—star milk

1. Hendrix
2. Dieterbaum
3. Mabinogian
4. Tolestoya
5. Acropolis
6. Serendipity
7. Ranawydal
8. Ogdanesso
9. Weverstine
10. Kowabonkers
11. Monongahela
12. Gort! Klaatu barada nikto

More Workouts

• Use any list of places, names, or specialized terms and do this same exercise. You can also try to see how many different sound-alike words or phrases you can develop for each word.

• Write down the last name of the following people: yourself, your best friend, your doctor, your pet (or an animal you know), a foreigner you admire, and a relative who does not have the same last name as you do. Perform the above exercise. Then examine each last name and its substitute word or phrase and determine if there is any connection that can be made between the person (or animal) and the substitute word or phrase. For example, my last name, Maguire, can be transposed into "mug, wire." I do, in fact, have a face that one might describe as a wiry mug. I have cup hooks in my kitchen that are, in a manner of speaking, mug wires. My name can also be transposed into "ma, choir"—and my mother sang for years in a church choir.

Exercise 5

Storyweaving: Remembering Lists by Spinning Stories

When I was a volunteer at a Harlem community center, I had the opportunity to observe very young kids experimenting with their own highly imaginative memory aids. One afternoon a four-year-old boy was playing with colored disks, and he wanted to remind himself of the pleasing order in which he had stacked them the day before. He began chanting to himself as he chose among the disks, "Blue, blue—looks like a shoe; red, red—shoe's on fire; yellow, yellow—it steps on an egg . . ."

Spinning a brief story that combines several items you want to remember is an excellent way of focusing on details and giving them associations. The storyweaving will also exercise your creativity, which may help you to achieve new insights into the material you are sorting out. Later, the flow of the narrative will help your mind summon up each desired item every time you turn your thoughts to the story.

Imagine that the words below refer to subjects you wish to discuss over the next few days. Weave a short story that contains all the terms, in the sequence they appear below. Underline each term as you write it down.

EXAMPLE:

fish
integrity
newspaper
campaign
necklace

Story: A <u>fish</u> was running for president of the ocean on a platform of <u>integrity</u>. When she read in the <u>newspaper</u> that her <u>campaign</u> manager had stolen a <u>necklace</u>, she was furious.

1.	fatherhood	6.	song
2.	vegetable	7.	lighthouse
3.	pipe organ	8.	triangle
4.	sneezing	9.	eraser
5.	carpet		

Story:

_____

_____

_____

_____

_____

_____

_____

_____

More Workouts

• Repeat the previous exercise, using any list of words you wish to remember. Try to compose as brief a story as you can.

• Many popular memory systems designed to retain sequence among individual items are based on associating each number with a strong visual image that sounds like the number it represents. These are commonly known as paired-associate systems. One such system for the numbers 1 through 10 is:

1.	sun	6.	sticks
2.	shoe	7.	heaven
3.	tree	8.	plate
4.	floor	9.	wine
5.	hive	10.	hen

Assume that you want to remember the following sequence of events: dust the furniture, take the cat to the vet, phone Dale, and prepare dinner. If you already have memorized the above system, you can first weave an image of a bun covered with dirt, then an image of a sickly Puss-in-Boots, then an image of Dale up a tree near phone wires, then a meal laid out on the floor. Later, simply by saying to yourself, "one, two, three, four," you will automatically conjure up these images and recollect the original events in their proper order.

Try the system out with your own list.

Mind Play

1. Create acrostics, acronyms, or catchphrases to record lists of items that are significant to you: for example, steps in a set of instructions; headings of a report or an article you wish to remember; ingredients in a recipe; personality qualities you want to cultivate; the names of exercises in this chapter.

2. Numbers are relatively devoid of sensory or associative content that would make them easier to remember. Given a long sequence of numbers, you can break it into parts and tackle each part separately; for example, 314625880 becomes 314-625-880. Or you can seek out relationships between the numbers. For example, *3 + 1 = 4*; double 3 and 1 and you have *6* and *2*; add 1 and 4 and you have *5*; *3 + 1 + 4 = 8* and *6 + 2 = 8*; subtract 8 from 8 and you have *0*.

A more intriguing way to remember phone numbers is to translate them into words according to the corresponding numbers on the dial or buttons of a telephone:

$$2 = ABC$$
$$3 = DEF$$
$$4 = GHI$$
$$5 = JKL$$
$$6 = MNO$$
$$7 = PRS$$
$$8 = TUV$$
$$9 = XYZ$$

(For "1," you can say "start" and for "0" you can say "stop.")

Thus, 864-2676 becomes UNICORN. Some numbers yield more than one word or phrase. Others do not yield any intelligible word or phrase, in which case you can create an acrostic. For instance, 858-2237 can be remembered by the phrase *"Too late to buy a dinner plate."* Experiment with your own telephone number and other telephone numbers you want to remember.

3. Choose a picture that contains numerous objects. List each object, and when you are finished, go back to the picture and point to each object on your list. Then lay the list and the picture aside and attempt to re-create the drawing on a blank sheet of paper. Compare your completed drawing with the original drawing and your list to determine how successful you were in remembering details. Try this exercise with different pictures.

More Memory Exercises

• Look through a photograph album. Study each picture and try to recall the events of the time it represents—especially, if possible, the day it was taken or the day you received it.

If you are in the photograph, try to recall how you felt at the time, physically and emotionally. If you are not in the photograph but someone else you know is, how would you characterize your relationship with this person at that time? If it is a black and white photograph, what would it look like in color?

If you have an old high school or college yearbook, focus on three or four portraits and list as many "peg words" as you can to describe what you remember about that person. Preferably, these peg words should be single terms that will trigger recall of particular characteristics, events, or aspects of your relationship with the subject of the portrait.

• Listen to music that was popular in your past or music that contains special meaning for you. Keep mental track of the thoughts and memories inspired by the music and then record those thoughts and memories in an abbreviated list.

Memory Games

Throughout history, people have delighted in playing games to exercise their memories. The nature of such games in any one period reveals much about the mind-set of that period, including how information tended to be organized for retention and what mental feats were considered evidence of a good memory.

In the seventeenth century, the British scientist Sir Francis Bacon designed his house at Gorhanbury to be a "memory theatre." Plants and animals were painted in windowpanes, and visitors were challenged to proceed through the house along a route that would arrange the flora and fauna in their proper biological categories. This was in keeping with a general seventeenth-century emphasis on empirical classifications.

In the eighteenth century, an era of building empires and encyclopedias, political and scientific systems were formulated according to "correspondencies." British writer Dr. Samuel Johnson gathered friends together to trade "similarities." One person would offer a quote or a fact and the others would be pressed to respond with a closely related quote or fact.

The nineteenth century witnessed a consolidation of history. The English-speaking world saw itself as the ultimate expression of the progress of time. The American writer Mark Twain invented and marketed a game he called Mark Twain's Memory Builder. Played on a peg-board divided into one hundred squares for the years in a century, the game required participants to remember dates of worldwide "accessions" (to thrones and presidencies), "battles," and "minor events" (such as discoveries).

The twentieth century, by contrast, is an era marked by fragmentation, diversity, and relativity. Specific names, rather than classifications or dates, constitute the points around which memories tend to gather. Over 75 percent of the questions asked in Trivial Pursuit, the very popular board game testing memory, hinge on the recollection of particular people, incidents, titles, or terms.

• Browse through a book of lists and choose a list that interests you, such as the names of people who made significant contributions to art or science before they were twenty-one or after they were seventy; the countries with the highest standard of living; or the most desired attributes in a mate or colleague. Use one or more of the memory exercises in this chapter—or adapt one of them—to register this list permanently in your mind.

The remembered list will serve as a framework for assembling and retaining additional information on the subject that you come across in the future. It may also help you out when you are at a loss for conversational material or when you want something neutral to contemplate while you are waiting for an appointment (the "stuck in a foxhole overnight" situation).

• One of the most important lessons I learned teaching literature classes is that rereading a well-liked book is not boring or a waste of time. On the contrary, it is a revelation. After four semesters of teaching Dostoevsky's *Crime and Punishment* and four rereadings of that novel at three-month intervals, the fifth rereading not only revived memories associated both directly and indirectly with past readings, but it also offered an entirely new experience of the book even richer than previous experiences.

Try rereading one of your favorite books. Begin with a book you have not read in a long time.

• Choose a favorite short poem or prose passage and commit it to memory, using any combination of the exercises offered in this chapter.

• Top executives in many corporations employ a bulletin-board memory technique to ensure that they do not forget to consider major issues they face, in either the performance of their general responsibilities or the handling of a particular multifaceted project.

If you have an office or work space, choose different areas of a nearby wall and associate each area with a different aspect of your job. Visualize a key word or image representing each aspect at the top of the particular spot you have assigned to it. You may want to imagine each wall section as a separate bulletin board on which you can mentally pin various notes, postcards, or sheets of paper that symbolize items falling within that area.

Simply turning to one of the wall areas occasionally will help you to focus your thoughts on the particular aspect of your work that the area represents. You can also add another detail to that area for each new thought or piece of information that relates to that aspect of your work.

• Choose a subject in your past that you wish to recall: your early childhood; your health patterns; your 1979 sojourn on the Baja peninsula; your Uncle Edgar.

Write down key phrases to organize what you can recall simply by thinking about that subject. Then write down ways in which you could enhance your memory of that subject, such as talking with other people, looking up pictures or maps, checking old records, writing letters, going to the library.

Pursue as many of these research strategies as you can, and keep track of what new memories this research effort triggers.

• Think of a category that represents one of your interests or concerns, such as "willpower," "breakthroughs in relationships," "grooming aids," or "old wives' tales," or think of a category that is fairly arbitrary, such as "things that are orange," "wolves," or "unusual noises."

The next day, take mental note of everything you experience that relates in some way to that category, such as conversations with other people, street occurrences, television programs, images in dreams, or specific physical or emotional sensations.

At the end of the day, make a list of these mental notes and see if they inspire any thoughts or revive any other memories that relate to the category you chose.

• The next time you are relaxing with friends or relatives, play the "pass-it-along" game. Whisper an idea or story into the ear of one person, and ask him or her to transfer the same story in the same manner to another person and so on, until everyone has participated. Then ask the last person to recount what he or she heard and compare it to the original version. It is almost always surprising and amusing to realize how different the last rendition is from the first.

• Write a letter to yourself incorporating all the things that happened to you during the day and how you felt about them. Seal the letter and put it aside for two weeks. Then, before reopening the letter, try to reconstruct what it says. Compare what you write down to what you wrote two weeks previously. Ask yourself why you may have forgotten or reinterpreted individual items.

• Experiment with devising and using external memory systems:

1. Using a single notebook, a box of index cards, or a drawer of folders, create a file system with

alphabetical categories representing subjects that interest you or that constitute major areas of your work and way of life. As you come across information that relates to one of these areas, you can save it for later review.

2. Keep a "commonplace book"—a blank notebook that you can divide into alphabetical sections with tabs that protrude beyond the pages. When you read or hear something that you want to remember, give it a one-word title and jot it down under the section indicated by the first letter of that word. You do not need to file items in order within an individual alphabetical section, and you can repeat titles when appropriate. The act of reviewing all the *A*'s, for example, to locate a quote entitled "Anxiety" that you once wrote down can refresh your memory about a number of different items and may cause you to run across an entry closely related to your "Anxiety" entry that you had forgotten.

3. Maintain a daily or weekly journal, being careful to record a range of items for each single event to increase the chance of your being able to recall it vividly at a later date. For example, if you went jogging in the morning, you may want to include what you thought about while you jogged, whom you passed, anything special that day about the landscape you crossed, how you felt before and after you jogged. You never know what your internal Sergeant Friday character will consider to be valuable information one month later. You may want to devote the entire journal to a theme: conversations you had during the day; your thoughts about a particular subject, like "children"; or progress reports regarding your work, your health, or your personal campaign toward reaching a specific goal.

4. Create a "to do" list for each day—either the night before or in the morning. Keep the entries simple: They need only spark your memory. Practice categorizing items according to priority, sequence, or similarity and committing them to memory. Each day, review the previous day's list to see if some items still need attention.

Analysis
Workouts

In its 1983 report "Educating Americans for the 21st Century," the National Science Board Commission on Precollege Education in Mathematics, Science and Technology says undeveloped analytical skills are most responsible for the decline in scholastic performance during the past fifteen years among students in the United States. The report goes on to call the "rush for a solution" one of the major contributors to this underdevelopment. In other words, our educational system so strongly pressures students to come up with a "right" answer to a problem that students are not devoting enough time and energy to such vital preliminary steps as understanding and redefining the problem, determining all of its ramifications, forming intelligent and imaginative hypotheses about it, and estimating and evaluating the full range of potential outcomes.

The average college graduate has taken over twenty-six hundred tests, quizzes, and examinations during his or her years of schooling, according to Dr. Roger von Oech, president of Creative Think, a California-based consulting firm. In almost all of these tests, quizzes, and examinations, the student is only required to record or select a "right" answer. Rarely is the student asked to describe how he or she reached the answer.

Our formal education encourages us to believe, consciously or unconsciously, that there is only one correct solution to a problem, that there is only one correct way of reaching that solution, and that there is no need to consider the problem further once we have come up with a correct solution. We forget that the process of coming to answers is more important to our intellectual growth than the answers themselves.

Even more alarming, we tend to consider every situation that begs for an answer as "a problem" and every problem as something that needs to be "solved." We use the expression *problem-solving skills* when we mean *analytical skills,* that is, skills that can be applied to opportunities as well as problems, and skills that enable us to comprehend, manage, rectify, and/or improve situations that are not by nature "solvable."

Because real-life situations are usually far more ambiguous and complex than the situations on examinations, our analytical skills are even more crucial outside the classroom than in it. If we are faced with a difficult work assignment, for example, we are faced with both a problem ("I don't know what to do") and an opportunity ("I can learn a lot by tackling it"). Uncertain that there is any single correct answer or any single correct procedure for reaching an answer, we need to draw on our previous experience, form tentative estimates, study possibilities, and test the hypotheses by trial and error. The same goes for difficulties in personal relationships.

Even such a seemingly clear-cut situation as a leaky ceiling is best handled with careful, skillful analysis. The problem, after all, is not the leaky ceiling, but a broken pipe or a clogged drain or a spillover in an upstairs room or too much snow or rain on the roof or a hole in the roof or a humidity imbalance in the building. All of these possibilities, plus the size, age, and nature of the leak itself, need to be considered. If they are not, we may find ourselves fixing the leak again and again without addressing the real problem. By analyzing before we act, we may even approach dealing with the leak as an opportunity to do some long-postponed but long-desired work, such as repainting or redesigning the ceiling or better insulating the roof.

Analysis takes patience, to be sure, but the rewards are well worth it. We may get much more immediate gratification from doing than thinking, but a feeling of ongoing satisfaction and achievement only comes from realizing that we have done things thoughtfully, utilizing our abilities to the best of their potential. To whatever degree we fail to appreciate this, because of our experience in school, in our heart of hearts we know it is so. How else can we explain our fascination with such archetypal analyzers as Robinson Crusoe, Sherlock Holmes, Hercule Poirot, Jane Marple, and Mr. Spock? Some part of us recognizes that being a good analyzer is not only essential for survival but fun as well.

Today, we possess technology to assist us in our analytical efforts that Crusoe, Holmes, Poirot, and Marple never had (we have yet to catch up with the technology of Mr. Spock's world!). Computers and calculators, however, have enhanced rather than diminished the value of our own analytical abilities. We have to feed appropriate data into these machines before they can perform any meaningful computations. We need to be able to estimate the probable results of those computations in advance, so that we will know if the answers are accurate. Otherwise, the machines are worthless.

The exercises in this chapter will enhance your ability to make reasonably correct estimates and approximations, to distinguish among parts of a whole, to establish rationales for circumstances and behaviors, and to formulate practical hypotheses that can assist you in addressing problems and opportunites.

Psych-up

I Know What I Like

As a college English teacher, whenever I asked students what they thought about an assigned text, they almost always responded either "I liked it" or "I didn't like it." Even after spending days trying to elicit more objective analyses of a work, I would still run up against this type of automatic, categorical yes or no evaluation. An entire month of discussion regarding Nathaniel Hawthorne's *The Scarlet Letter,* for example, would yield essays that began, "I would have hated living in colonial Massachusetts."

We all instinctively divide our experiences into those we enjoy and those we do not enjoy. If a friend solicits our opinion about a movie we saw, most likely our review will be organized around whether we found it pleasurable or not. When we meet someone new, it is difficult to avoid considering first and foremost whether we approve of that person. Behavioral scientists tell us that we form a lasting impression about a new acquaintance within four minutes after initial contact—an impression that is no more consciously precise than "okay" or "not okay" and that stands a 50 percent chance of being wrong.

By not exploring the reasons why we like or dislike a person, place, or thing, we prevent ourselves not only from learning more about that person, place, or thing but also from learning more about how and why we act and think the way we do. By becoming more attuned to what gives us pleasure or pain, we can grow intellectually and emotionally and gain control over the quality and content of our lives.

Read each description listed below and think of an example from your own experience. Then provide as many specific reasons as you can for your attitude.

1. A person I hate:

_____

_____

_____

_____

2. A fictional character I love:

_____

_____

_____

_____

3. An activity I enjoy:

_____

_____

_____

_____

4. A food I dislike:

_____

_____

_____

_____

5. A famous person I admire:

_____

_____

_____

_____

6. An experience that disappointed me:

_____

_____

_____

_____

We cannot keep ourselves from forming opinions about whether we like or dislike people, places, or things: It is an instinct and, like all instincts, can work toward self-preservation. What we can do, however, is defer our final judgment and base it on analysis rather than instinct. Certainly instincts need to be considered in that analysis, but so do many other factors. Otherwise, we are reacting as animals and not acting as human beings. We may share 98 percent of our genes with the chimpanzees, but that extra 2 percent that gives us our unique cortical brain structure—enabling us to analyze data more rationally and logically—makes all the difference!

Among factors other than the like/dislike instinct that need to be considered are the following:

1. What in your previous experience may be influencing your opinion about a newly encountered subject? You may, for example, dislike a person because he or she is wearing a scent exactly like the scent worn by someone you disliked. You may enjoy a movie because it features a house exactly like the one you cherish from childhood.

2. What circumstances surrounding your encounter with a particular subject may be influencing your opinion? You may, for example, be predisposed to enjoy a place you visit solely because it represents a timely escape from a place you do not want to be. You may dislike a book because you are being compelled to read it or because the print is taxing on your eyes.

3. What in your own personality or lifestyle influences your opinion about a particular subject? You may dislike someone because that person has inadvertently witnessed one of your "bad" qualities. You may form a negative attitude about a specific food because it is not part of your regular diet.

Knowing everything that accounts for our reactions to individual persons, places, or things helps us ensure that our final judgments about them will be not only fair but also productive. It is especially helpful if we can begin to recognize patterns among our reactions so that we can avoid being at the mercy of bad habits or ignorance and derive more satisfaction from all of the experiences life gives us.

More Psych-ups

• Follow the same procedure with any person, place, or thing you like or dislike. You may find it most convenient to review the past day or week for subject matter, concentrating on fresh experiences. From time to time, however, you also need to focus on long-standing likes and dislikes, ones that will put more pressure on you to be objective.

• For variety, try performing this psych-up from the point of view of someone else. Pick a family member or a friend and think of what he or she likes and dislikes. Try to analyze why this person feels the way he or she does about each item.

Exercise 1

Time, Space, and Mass: Estimating Numbers

Situations in everyday life call more often for approximate numbers than exact numbers. Estimation, not actual computation, provides answers to such questions as "Can I afford to buy a new coat?"; "Will this chair fit in my bedroom?"; "When should I leave home to get to my appointment on time?"; "How many spectators are watching this game?"; "Will this food be enough for six people?"

Most of us feel we are not very good at estimating, probably because of our experience in mathematics classes, where exact numbers are almost always demanded. Accustomed to believing that an exact answer is the only "real" or "worthwhile" answer, we are apt to feel uncomfortable committing ourselves to an imprecise calculation. The more we experiment in making estimates, however, the better we get and the more we appreciate that a good estimate is usually all we need.

Systematically practicing estimation skills helps develop a general sense of numbers. We learn to interpret statistical data, charts, and graphs with more understanding and to judge durations, distances, dimensions, quantities, and proportions more effectively. But perhaps the most important benefit is the increase in our overall practical knowledge that results from continually making "guesstimates" about the world around us.

Answer each question. Don't do any calculations, and use whatever units of measurement you wish (for instance, miles, feet, yards, or blocks for distances). Remember that any answer is better than no answer. Guessing plays a major role in estimating.

EXAMPLE:

How long does it take to cook an average dinner at home?   40 minutes

How far is it from your home to the nearest clothing store?   2 miles

What is the size of the building in which you live?   60 feet long, by 40 feet wide, by 20 feet high

What object within your present range of vision weighs closest to 25 pounds?   the black chair

How much of the average day do you spend sleeping?   one third

watching television?   10 percent

Duration

1. How much time would it take you to walk to the nearest drugstore? _____

2. How much time does it take to play the average record album? _____

3. How much time does it take you to read 100 printed pages? _____

4. How long does the sun stay up on an average day in June? _____
in December? _____

5. How long has it been since the last time you laughed so hard it hurt? _____

Distance

1. How long is the route to the nearest bathroom? _____

2. How wide is the street on which you live? _____

3. How long is your average stride? _____

4. How much ground do you cover in an average day? _____

5. How far is it from Boston to Washington, D.C.? _____
from New York to Chicago? _____
from Miami to Dallas? _____
from St. Louis to Denver? _____
from Los Angeles to Seattle? _____

Dimensions

1. What is the area of the room you occupy? _____

2. How much closet space do you have where you live? _____

3. How big is the bed in which you sleep? _____

4. How tall is the tallest building in your community? _____

5. What is the size of this book? _____

Quantities

1. What is the population of your city or town? _____

2. How many books do you read in a year? _____

3. How much do the clothes you are wearing weigh? _____

4. How much water would it take to completely fill your kitchen sink? _____

5. What *one* item would you buy if you were allowed to spend $100? _____
$500? _____
$5,000? _____
$25,000? _____
$1,000,000? _____

Proportions

1. Given the colors yellow, red, green, and blue, which occupies the least amount of space within your range of vision? _____

2. What proportion of total space in the room you occupy is taken up by furniture? _____

3. On what percentage or fraction of phone calls that you make do you receive a busy signal? __

4. What percentage or fraction of the average day do you spend alone? _____

5. What percentage or fraction of the movies you see are comedies? _____
   dramas? _____
   fantasy, science-fiction, and horror films? _____
   documentaries or filmed performance events? _____

More Workouts

• Perform this same exercise, substituting a different item (where appropriate) for the one (or ones) specified in each question. This requires using your imagination to rephrase the question as well as your estimation abilities to answer it.

• Focus on a single room or place and its contents and apply the appropriate questions from each category.

• Focus on one unit of measurement: a week, an inch, a dollar, a square foot, a pound, a given percentage or fraction (such as 50 percent or one third). Formulate estimation questions based on applying your chosen unit of measurement to different subjects.

For example, given "a week," you may want to estimate the percentage of time you spend performing different activities in an average week or the amount of money you will spend on different types of things in the course of two weeks. Given the fraction one third, you may want to pose to yourself such questions as "What different tasks could I eliminate during the day to give me one-third more time?"; "What objects would I choose to sacrifice in the living room to give me one-third more space?"; "Given all the objects on my table, how could I divide them into three piles that would each weigh the same?"

• It is not necessary to check out the accuracy of individual estimates to derive benefit from a numerical estimation exercise. The whole point is simply to involve you in the process of numerical estimation. The more you experiment with it in your own life, the more conversant you will become with numbers and the sharper your sense of duration, distance, dimension, quantity, and proportion will be.

Nevertheless, every now and then it is wise to make a few estimates that you can easily check out just for the fun of seeing how close you can come to the "correct" answers. Estimations regarding the size of rooms and objects, the distance between different geographical points, the population of different cities, states, and countries, and the number of words in a given amount of text space are examples of estimates that are relatively easy to verify.

Estimating Proportions

What percentage (or fraction) of each box is shaded?

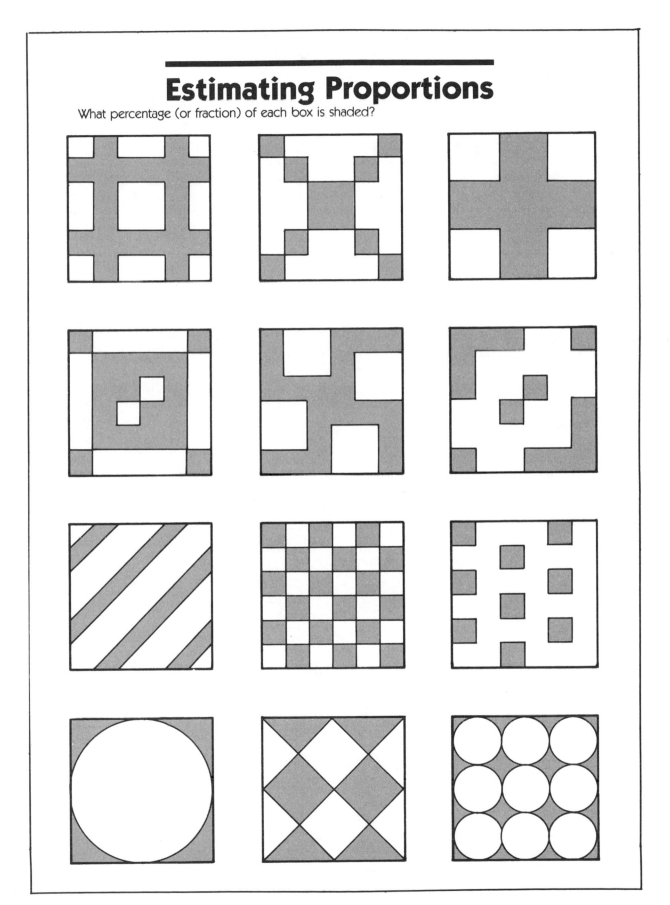

Exercise 2

Divide and Conquer: Examining the Parts of a Whole

In 1957, shortly after directing and starring in the film *The Prince and the Showgirl,* Sir Laurence Olivier had a long conversation about his acting technique with Arthur Miller. "Before deciding on what approach I will take to a character," Olivier claimed, "I go through a complete mental breakdown."

Taken out of context, Olivier's remark suggests that he endures an extreme but understandable crisis of nerves before each of his always fascinating performances. Taken in context, however, his remark more likely means that he analyzes each and every aspect of a character to determine how best to portray that character to an audience.

The word *analysis* comes from the Greek word *analyein,* which means "to break down." Only by figuratively breaking down a whole into its parts and carefully considering each of these parts can we fully comprehend that whole, whether it be a person, a place, an event, a relationship, an abstract topic, or a concrete object. Ray Bradbury, author of numerous science fiction stories and novels, offers some very useful advice for improving our analytical skill in this manner: "Pretend you are an intelligent being from another planet when you look at the world around you. Pick one particular thing that catches your eye and imagine you had to report everything you could about that thing to your superiors back home. You will find that what once seemed obvious becomes fascinating and what once seemed mysterious becomes clear."

Note the categories listed under each of the items below. Put something in each category, even if you have to guess. Do not worry about covering everything in each category; be as comprehensive or selective as you wish. Following each category, under the heading "Similarities," list other items that share one or more of the same characteristics.

EXAMPLE:

Ohio

definition: (as in an encyclopedia): a state in the midwestern United States, roughly square (about 200 miles by 200 miles), with about 11 million inhabitants, bounded on the north by Lake Erie and Michigan, on the east by Pennsylvania and West Virginia, on the South by West Virginia and Kentucky, and on the west by Indiana

similarities: Illinois (in population and size); a chevron or a shield (in shape); New York (also bordered on the north by a Great Lake; Iowa (a word for a state consisting of four letters, each of which can be reversed and still retain it original configuration)

major cities: Cleveland, Columbus, Cincinnati, Dayton, Akron, and Toledo *similarities*:   Spain also has a city named Toledo; Indiana, Georgia, and Nebraska also have cities named Columbus; the District of Columbia was carved out of the center of the United States in the late eighteenth century to be the site of the nation's capital, whereas Columbus was carved out of the center of Ohio to be the state's capital; Cincinnati is very much like St. Louis—it was a nineteenth-century "gate to the west," lies on the extended Mississippi River system, has about the same population, and was settled largely by German-speaking people

famous natives: Ulysses S. Grant, William McKinley, William Howard Taft, Warren G. Harding, the Wright Brothers, Thomas Edison, John Glenn

similarities: Virginia is also the birthplace of many U.S. presidents; Alexander Graham Bell is another famous American inventor who, like Edison, produced many advancements in technology involving electricity; Eisenhower, like Grant, was an army general who became President

1. Light bulb

definition (as in a dictionary):

_____

_____

_____

_____

similarities:

_____

_____

_____

_____

structures:

_____

_____

_____

_____

similarities:

_____

_____

_____

_____

functions:

_____

_____

_____

_____

similarities:

_____

_____

_____

2. A close friend (supply a specific name)

description (as in a police blotter):

_____

_____

_____

_____

similarities:

_____

_____

_____

habits:

_____

_____

_____

_____

similarities:

_____

_____

_____

_____

clothing:

_____

_____

_____

_____

similarities:

_____

_____

_____

_____

"Each of a fact's associates becomes a hook to which it hangs, a means to fish it up when sunk beneath the surface."—William James

3. The expression "Haste makes waste"

explanation (as in a glossary of expressions):

_____

_____

_____

_____

similarities:

_____

_____

_____

_____

general situations to which it applies:

_____

_____

_____

_____

similarities:

_____

_____

_____

_____

specific related incidents from my own experience:

_____

_____

_____

similarities:

_____

_____

_____

_____

Comparative Estimates

a _____ b _____ c _____ | F | | G |

d _____

e _____

How many A's would it take to cover B?   C?   D?   E?
How many B's would it take to cover C?   D?   E?
How many C's would it take to cover D?   E?

How many F's would it take to cover G?   H?   I?   J?
How many G's would it take to cover I?   H?   J?
How many H's would it take to cover I?   J?

I

H   J

More Workouts

• This exercise provides partial models for analyzing a place (such as Ohio), an object (such as a light bulb), a person (such as a close friend), and an abstraction (such as the expression "Haste makes waste"). Perform the same exercise substituting different places, objects, people, or abstractions.

• Practice varying the categories. Here are some suggestions to get you started on thinking up your own:

1. *places*—history, recreational opportunities, physical features, famous associations, symbolic representations, potential for development

2. *objects*—material, color, taste, smell, sound, texture, dimension, weight, volume, durability, shape

3. *people*—beliefs, achievements, lifestyles, roles, past experiences, loved ones, favorite possessions, affiliations

4. *abstractions*—symbolic representations, historical illustrations, relevant areas of human experience (activities, states of being, professions, social and cultural events)
• Take any particular item—such as a place, object, person, or abstraction—and analyze it in terms of polarities, for example, positive aspects vs. negative aspects, known elements vs. unknown elements, or constants vs. variables.

• Practice becoming more and more comprehensive in your analysis as you go along. Work toward listing as many characteristics as you can under each category and as many similarities as you can for each characteristic. Try to give balanced attention to each category.

Exercise 3

Standing in the Other Person's Shoes: Appreciating Many Points of View

F. Scott Fitzgerald defined genius as "the art of entertaining two or more opposed ideas in mind at the same time and still maintaining the ability to function." As a novelist, Fitzgerald was predisposed to come up with this definition, for the challenge he repeatedly gave himself was the challenge every novelist faces: to create a cast of "opposed" characters, each of whom can function effectively as the spokesperson of a different life philosophy but who together can generate a unified story conveying the author's own particular philosophy.

Being able to identify and analyze different possible points of view regarding an item or situation not only helps us avoid becoming single-minded or habitual in our thinking, it also helps us work more effectively with others to solve problems and generate ideas that serve a common purpose. When we put ourselves in other people's shoes, we give ourselves new frameworks within which to exercise our analytical skills. We develop a broader understanding of whatever phenomenon we choose to examine, a fresher perspective on how our own thinking may appear to others, and more penetrating insights into other ways of thinking besides our own.

Consider each of the following items from the point of view of the person indicated. Note possible attitudes, opinions, motivations, and/or behaviors that are appropriate in each case.

EXAMPLE

Television:

an advertiser: would see television as a very expensive but very powerful marketing tool; would want to identify shows appealing to potential buyers of products or services; would be most interested in shows with a high percentage of viewers; would study commercials carefully

a child: would see television as a highly compelling source of entertainment and a potential source of information about the outside world; would be interested in shows with a lot of action and fantasy; would wonder what the people on television did inside the box when the set was off; would enjoy commercials almost as much as regular programming; would be very curious about shows on late at night and other programs that are "off limits"

an invalid: could find television the only comfortable source of entertainment and information—a means of keeping in touch with the world; could feel chained to television from time to time; could be depressed seeing people enjoying a wide range of activities that he or she could not perform; could be drawn to shows that feature characters coping with hardships (for example, soap operas); would probably see a wide range of shows and develop particular tastes among a variety of program types; could develop a real hatred for commercials *a teacher:*   could see television as a major mind waster, worrying about the essential passivity of the viewer; could also see television as having enormous educational potential, given the right leadership; would be especially interested in instructional and documentary programs as well as taped performances of cultural events; could resent feeling that he or she must perform in the classroom in the manner in which Johnny Carson or Joan Rivers performs; could find a few appropriate models for classroom delivery; widely viewed programs could be one of the few sources for lively class discussion

1. An employee is fired:

the employee who is fired:

_____

_____

_____

_____

a co-worker of the fired employee:

_____

_____

_____

_____

the boss who does the firing:

_____

_____

_____

_____

the employee's spouse:

_____

_____

_____

_____

the employee's neighbors:

_____

_____

_____

_____

2. A small, beautiful, historic but dilapidated apartment building faces demolition to make way for a large, boxlike hotel:

the apartment-building residents:

_____

_____

_____

_____

the city developers:

_____

_____

_____

_____

the hotel owners:

_____

_____

_____

_____

a preservationist committee:

_____

_____

3. Red:

a member of the Communist Party:

_____

_____

_____

_____

an interior decorator:

_____

_____

_____

a doctor:

_____

_____

_____

_____

an accountant:

_____

_____

_____

_____

an American Indian:

_____

_____

_____

4. A patron in a crowded restaurant has waited a long time for service:

the patron:

_____

_____

_____

_____

the waiter:

_____

_____

_____

the restaurant manager:

_____

_____

_____

_____

_____

a newspaper reporter:

_____

_____

_____

_____

5. A daughter announces her homosexuality to her mother and father:

the daughter:

_____

_____

_____

_____

the mother:

_____

_____

_____

_____

the father:

_____

_____

_____

_____

the daughter's homosexual friends:

_____

_____

_____

_____

the daughter's heterosexual friends:

_____

_____

_____

6. Success:

a businessperson:

_____

_____

_____

_____

a teenager:

_____

_____

_____

_____

a member of the clergy:

_____

_____

_____

_____

a sculptor:

_____

_____

_____

_____

More Workouts

• Repeat the exercise using any subject for which you can develop at least three different points of view. Crises within a workplace, a community, or a household lend themselves particularly well to this type of activity. If you pick a situation from your own experience, explore the points of view not only of the people involved, but also of others.

• As you develop proficiency, try sorting out the differences and similarities among various points of view. Then experiment with articulating "compromise" points of view—ones that might satisfy all or most of the parties involved.

• Perform this exercise using the same assortment of personality types for each item. Here are some sample assortments to get you started:

1. The rationalist, the romantic, the moralist, and the survivalist

2. The optimist, the pessimist, the conformist, and the nonconformist

3. The bull, the bear, the chicken, and the fox

"What is, for example, the attitude of different people toward a forest? A painter who has gone there to paint, the owner of the forest who wishes to evaluate his business prospects, an officer who is interested in the tactical problem of defending the area, a hiker who wants to enjoy himself. . . . While they can all agree to the abstract statement that they stand at the edge of a forest, the different kinds of activity they are set to accomplish will determine their experience of 'seeing a forest.' "—Erich Fromm

Exercise 4

Reasons That Rhyme: Forming Hypotheses

The philosopher René Descartes once said that what most distinguishes human intelligence from animal intelligence is the pursuit of the question "Why?"

We see this most markedly in preschool children, who have not yet been conditioned to accept limitations of their rational powers or to rely completely on books and authorities to provide logical explanations. A child hears thunder and immediately begins spinning possible theories to account for it: Angels are having a fight; clouds are banging into each other; a giant is walking across the sky; God is doing his laundry. The opinions of parents and playmates are solicited and considered, but usually the child persists in developing possible reasons until one of them is definitely revealed through his or her own experience as the "correct" one.

A successful adult analyst can continue to speculate with the freedom of a child and yet control any speculations by testing them systematically against all of his or her knowledge and experience. Formulating hypotheses about the nature of a phenomenon or situation, about the cause and solution of a problem, or about the source and extent of an opportunity helps us arrange the data we accumulate so that we can give direction to our thoughts and strategy to our research. The more hypotheses we generate, the more comprehensive and effective our analysis will be.

Develop as many hypotheses as you can (at least three) to account for each of the following situations. Remember to consider all possible reasons and not just the most probable ones.

EXAMPLE:

I have received no mail for four days.

• No one has written to me because I haven't written many letters myself or done anything lately to keep correspondence going.

• It is an especially busy time of year for people—no one has time to write.

• It is an especially slow time of year for people—no one has anything to say.

• It is a coincidence: All my correspondents are either sick or preoccupied or "between letters."

• A crisis at the post office is delaying the mail: a mail glut or a breakdown in equipment or an unexpected drop in staff.

• The regular mail carrier is ill or on vacation and the new one is inadvertently skipping me.

• The mail carrier is deliberately not giving me my mail; either he or she is spying on me or is mad at me for something (maybe my dog is a nuisance) or feels that leaving my mail at my home is unsafe or temporarily burdensome (maybe a note to this effect got lost).

• Someone is stealing my mail after it is delivered—either for a particular purpose (some enemy I have made or someone who has an interest in a particular item I may get in the mail) or simply as a prank.

1. A horse is wandering down the street where I live.

_____

_____

_____

_____

Mini Mysteries

Put your analyical skills to work on these mini mysteries. Possible solutions are printed on page 118.

Good-bye, Dear

A man kisses his wife before leaving for work, closes his apartment door, enters the elevator, pushes the button, and realizes immediately that his wife has died. What happened?

Island Murder

Five men spend one night on a deserted island. The next morning, the police find the murdered body of one of the men inside a clump of bushes, where it is obvious he has been struggling with someone else. The police arrest all four men and announce that they will know who the murderer is in twenty-four hours. How?

Dangling Sentence

A woman is arrested for murder, tried, found guilty, and sentenced to die; but the execution can never be carried out. Why?

Fifty-three Bicycles

A man is discovered one morning shot to death in a room with fifty-three bicycles. What happened?

2. Someone of the opposite sex who has never shown any interest in me suddenly goes out of his or her way to be friendly.

_____

_____

_____

_____

3. I turn a corner on a busy city street and suddenly almost everyone I see is wearing a flower.

_____

_____

_____

_____

4. I wake up at five o'clock in the morning for several days in a row.

_____

_____

_____

_____

5. I discover that an acquaintance of mine [supply the real name] has moved to Tahiti.

_____

_____

_____

_____

More Workouts

• Perform this same exercise with any "mysterious" phenomenon or situation in your recent or past experience.

• As you develop proficiency in performing this exercise, try inventing the most fanciful hypotheses you can. Consider, for example, possible science fiction explanations.

• From time to time, concentrate on one phenomenon or episode and develop more detailed scenarios organized around three different hypotheses. Also try arranging hypotheses in order of probability or listing the steps that you would need to take to investigate each one.

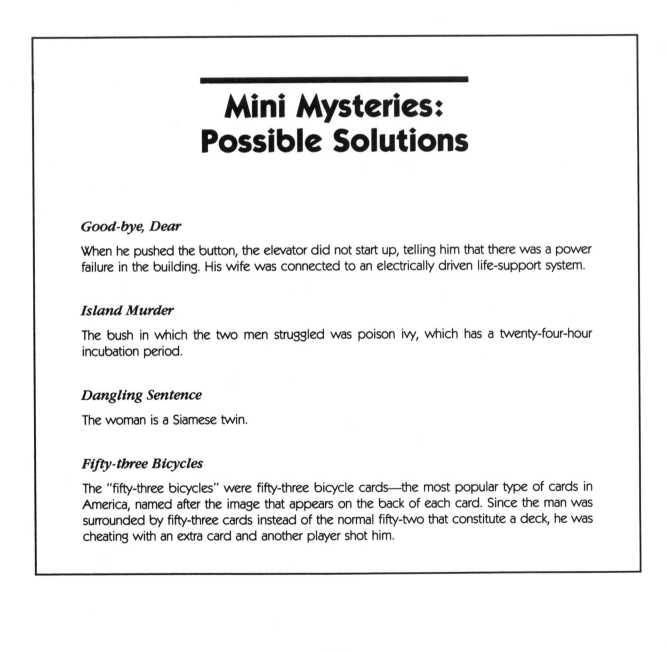

Mini Mysteries: Possible Solutions

Good-bye, Dear

When he pushed the button, the elevator did not start up, telling him that there was a power failure in the building. His wife was connected to an electrically driven life-support system.

Island Murder

The bush in which the two men struggled was poison ivy, which has a twenty-four-hour incubation period.

Dangling Sentence

The woman is a Siamese twin.

Fifty-three Bicycles

The "fifty-three bicycles" were fifty-three bicycle cards—the most popular type of cards in America, named after the image that appears on the back of each card. Since the man was surrounded by fifty-three cards instead of the normal fifty-two that constitute a deck, he was cheating with an extra card and another player shot him.

Mind Play

1. Take a single word and, using any combination of individual letters in that word, create as many different words as you can. As you become more accomplished, experiment with "transpositions": short phrases made by rearranging all the letters in a single word. Here are some examples:

ignorant	=	Grin, O ant.
neighbors	=	our big hens
admirable	=	a mild bear
astronomers	=	moon starers
revolution	=	to love ruin
Great Britain	=	I bring a treat

Either of these activities can also be performed by two or more people as a game.

2. Take a single word and compose as precise a definition as you can, one that you might find in a dictionary. Then list synonyms and antonyms of that word.

With groups of four or more people, you can create you own version of the game Dictionary, based on either of these approaches:

• A different leader in each round chooses a word from a dictionary that no one knows. The leader pronounces it and spells it but does not read the definition. Instead, he or she writes down the definition on a slip of paper, attaching his or her initials. Each of the other players writes down his or her own definition for the word on a slip of paper, noting his or her initials. The leader collects the slips of paper and reads the definitions. Each person picks the definition that he or she feels is the correct one. Individual players get one point for picking the correct definition and one point for each person who picks his or her definition as the correct one. The leader gets one point for every wrong answer.

• A different leader in each round chooses a word he or she feels that none of the other players will know, tells them what the first letter is, and reads only the definition. Then he or she writes down the correct word on a slip of paper, attaching his or her initials. Each of the other players writes down a word on a slip of paper to fit the definition, using the same first letter and noting his or her initials. The leader collects the slips and reads the words. Individual players get one point for picking the correct word and one point for each person who picks his or her word as the correct one. The leader gets one point for every wrong answer.

3. Acquire games that will enable you to exercise your analytical powers regularly. Crossword puzzles can be found in newspapers and magazines as well as special crossword puzzle books. Numerous books containing logic puzzles, brainteasers, mathematical games, riddles, and mini-mysteries are widely available at newsstands and in bookstores. Many boxed games can be played either alone or in groups: for example, Leisure Time Games' Facts in Five and Selchow and Righter's Sentence Cube Game and Scrabble.

4. While you are reading mystery stories or watching mystery dramas on televison, write down clues and hypotheses, both the ones that characters note and the ones that you yourself perceive. Try to reach a solution before it is actually presented. Experiment with different ways of organizing and arranging data.

5. Think of a story you know well—based on a novel, a short story, a fairy tale, a play, a television show, or a movie—and briefly rewrite that story from the point of view of some character other than the main one. Adapt original scenes or add new ones to render the character you have chosen the new main character.

Logic Games

Four athletes are gathered around a table at a resort, talking about their respective sports. Here is what we know about where each one is sitting:

    The golfer is sitting across from Mike.

    The jogger is sitting on the swimmer's right.

    Mark is sitting across from the tennis player.

    Molly is sitting on Mary's left.

    There is a man sitting on Mike's right.

What is each person's sport?

Eight cards have been numbered and lie face down in this arrangement:

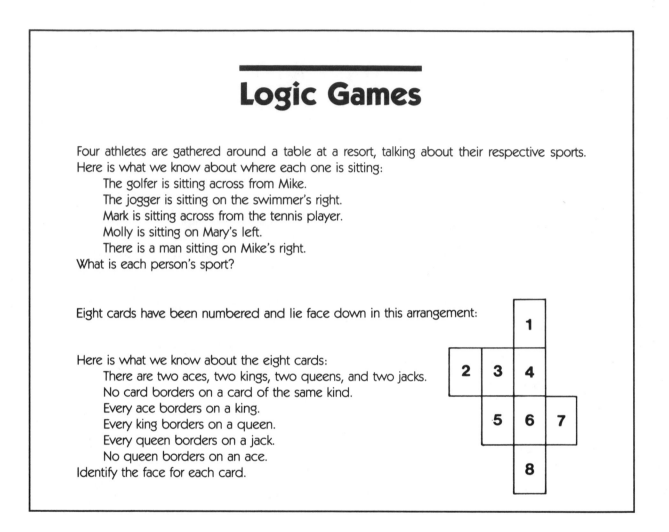

Here is what we know about the eight cards:

    There are two aces, two kings, two queens, and two jacks.

    No card borders on a card of the same kind.

    Every ace borders on a king.

    Every king borders on a queen.

    Every queen borders on a jack.

    No queen borders on an ace.

Identify the face for each card.

More Analysis Exercises

• Choose some aspect of your life or your environment that contains a lot of quantifiable, measurable data: your business, your wardrobe, your daily time schedule, your art collection, your diet, your hobby. Create different types of charts (for example, flowcharts, pie charts, symbols of various shapes, sizes, and colors), graphs (for example, bar graphs, graphs using two axes, graphs divided into equal-sized squares), and diagrams (for example, outlines, branching diagrams, circular diagrams, maps) to communicate the following things:

    • the different categories or classifications into which you can organize data

    • any relative durations, distances, dimensions, quantities, or proportions you can establish among data that fall within or among any of these categories, for the purpose of more easily comparing and contrasting that data

- any specific processes or procedures pertaining to that aspect of your life

• Experiment with learning as much as you can about, or with, a specific analytical tool. Try different types of operations with a calculator, a computer, a tape measure, a scale, a compass, measuring cups and spoons. Make estimates before actually determining answers.

• Draw up sets of plans (budgets, procedures, schedules, scenarios) based on your analysis of a particular aspect of your life or environment. For example, consider different possible furniture arrangements for your living room, or plan possible ways to enhance a relationship.

• Pay close attention to any patterns you observe in the course of a single day, for example, habits in your behavior or the behavior of others, designs that recur in different advertisements for the same type of product, similarities in the kinds of expressions that you or others repeatedly use, rhythms in the ebb and flow of traffic through a specific area over a specific period of time.

• Pick a general subject involving a lot of numerical data that interests you and is routinely featured in a newspaper: for example, sports, cooking, the stock market, plants, or home maintenance and design. Follow this subject over a period of time, devising and applying different methods for exercising your analytical skills.

Suppose, for example, that you choose the stock market. You may decide to follow the ups and downs of particular stocks from day to day. If you select cooking, you can estimate ways to vary recipes or calculate how much money you will save using coupons.

• Cultivate a talent you possess involving tools and estimates: drawing, painting, playing racquetball, woodworking, photography, sewing. Develop your talent by analyzing durations, distances, dimensions, quantities, and proportions.

• Develop your own special code for the letters in the alphabet. Use this code to write down something that you especially want to think about (it will indirectly help you concentrate on it) or something that is very private (it will provide you with a "safe" record). Here are some ideas for code systems to get you started:

  - Transpose successive pairs of letters in the alphabet: "a" will stand for "b" and "b" for "a"; "c" will stand for "d" and "d" for "c"; and so forth.
  - Write the alphabet backward and give each letter a number: "z" = 1, "y" = 2, and so forth. Use the numbers to represent the letters in your code.
  - Choose a short poem, a well-known expression, or a passage from a book and write it out. Below each letter in order, write the letter in the alphabet in order for which it will stand. Pass over repeated letters in the original. When most of the letters have already been used up in the original and some letters remain uncoded (for example, "s" through "z"), you can stop and simply not bother using code for the remaining letters. Suppose, for instance, that you choose the beginning of Lincoln's Gettysburg Address. Correspondences will work as follows:

    ```
    original:  F o u r   s c o r e   a n d   s e v e n . . .
    code:      a b c d   e f - - g   h i j   - - k - l . . .
    ```

  - Invent your own symbolic characters for each of the letters in the alphabet: for example, "*" = a, "#" = b, and so forth.

7
Decision-making Workouts

After the American hostages in Iran were released in January 1981, media reporters barraged them with questions about what it was like to spend over a year in captivity. Many agreed that the worst aspect of the experience was the lack of any scope for personal decision-making. "At first, I would go over and over what could be done to get us out of there," one ex-hostage explained, "until I thought I'd go nuts. Instead, I began deciding what I'd think about each day, what words I would use, how I would act if certain things happened, what I would do when I got back home." Survivors of World War II concentration and prisoner-of-war camps, people who have been kidnapped, victims of serious illnesses who have endured lengthy convalescences, and former prison inmates have reported similar frustrations that left them with a heightened appreciation of the power to make decisions.

It does not take a major life trauma, however, for us to understand how much we count on being able to make decisions. Whenever a moment comes along when we are compelled to wait for events to happen to us instead of exercising control over those events, we feel a touch of what it must be like to be a hostage, a victim of illness or kidnapping, or a prisoner. Even the mere suggestion of such a situation can elicit a strong response.

One Saturday morning I witnessed my seven-year-old godchild realize this dilemma as we watched cartoons on television together. Thanks to the machinations of his archfoes the Beagle Boys, Donald Duck was stranded on a treeless tropical islet only a little bigger than he was—without food or tools and, most discouragingly of all, without Huey, Dewey, and Louie and their miracle worker, *The Junior Woodchuck's Handbook*. Right away he threw himself into building a shelter from the sun with his shirt; but then the only thing he could do was sit in the shade, covering himself with his hands (Donald, shirtless, is unusually modest considering that he never wears pants). "Decisions, decisions, everywhere," Donald squawked, "and not a one to make." My godchild laughed nervously. He understood what Donald meant.

We make so many decisions every day that we can wind up taking them for granted: "What shall I wear today?" "How shall I respond in this conversation?" "What shall I have for lunch?" "What shall I do with this hundred-dollar surplus?" Indeed, almost everything we do is the result of a decision, whether we are consciously aware of having made one or not.

For centuries, people never paid much attention to how decisions are made, nor did they develop any formulas for improving one's decision-making skills. Some folks seemed better at making decisions than others, and this was attributed to natural talent. It appeared obvious that one should do what one thinks is best and that one should examine all the facts before making a decision, but that is as far as any guidelines went. Each decision was considered unique. One merely made a decision—sometimes based on a value system, sometimes not—or a decision would inevitably be made for one.

The nineteenth century saw a significant change in how the Western world viewed decision-making. Drawing on newly developed scientific methodologies, businesspeople began following standard procedures for reaching the most effective decisions. The insurance industry, for example, grew rapidly as underwriters were able to rely more and more successfully on probability tables created by mathematicians and actuaries. In 1832, Charles Babbage, the first person to attempt to build a large practical computer, founded a new science of decision-making based on arranging data according to where "points of choice" lay.

In the 1930s and 1940s, governments dealing with worldwide depression and war drafted or hired large numbers of scientists, educators, and "thinking experts" to study decision-making. The result has been an ongoing flood of decision-making theories (decisions of certainty vs. uncertainty vs. risk; decisions of policy vs. contingency vs. initiative; programmed decisions vs. decisions of encounter), management science techniques (cost-benefit determination; management by objectives; synectics; brainstorming), and whole new areas of decision-making endeavors (operations research; quality control; strategic planning; life-work goal setting).

Miles Hickock, director of Merrimack Research Associates, remarks, "Over the past 150 years we have acquired a more precise definition of what decision-making involves and a general process model for making better decisions that has completely revolutionized our decision-making capabilities. It is somewhat like what is just starting to happen now in the case of 'creativity.'"

What, then, is this definition? And what is this process model?

Decision-making is the act of commitment to one alternative among all possible alternatives. What is important about this definition is its emphasis on decision-making as an *action* fundamentally based on *assumption,* rather than a *reaction* to *facts.* Effective decision-making is future-oriented and requires exercising both intuitive and analytical skills. Each well-made decision begins with a theory, checks the data, and ends with a judgment.

Every source on the subject recommends following a clear process in order to arrive at a decision. Doing this helps the decision come more easily and ensures the most favorable results. It also enables us to broaden our understanding of different decision-making environments so that we can make increasingly more intelligent and informed decisions in the future.

Virtually all published models follow these steps for making a good decision:

1. Define the basic problem or opportunity involved.

2. Identify or establish overall goals that will be met or advanced by making a decision.

3. Develop decision criteria from these goals: specific, measurable results that you want to achieve by making a decision.

4. Research the "decision environment": details pertaining to the subject of the decision as well as opportunities and constraints facing you, given all relevant resources and developments both inside and outside your control.

5. Establish choices.

6. Estimate the extent to which each alternative satisfies or does not satisfy the decision criteria by applying an appropriate system of measurement.

7. Choose the alternative that best fulfills the decision criteria.

8. Devise ways to implement the decision so that the effects of the decision can be evaluated.

The exercises in this chapter are designed to enhance your decision-making abilities by giving you practice in stating the purpose of a decision, in gathering and evaluating data affecting a decision, in building models to clarify decision choices, and in executing a final decision.

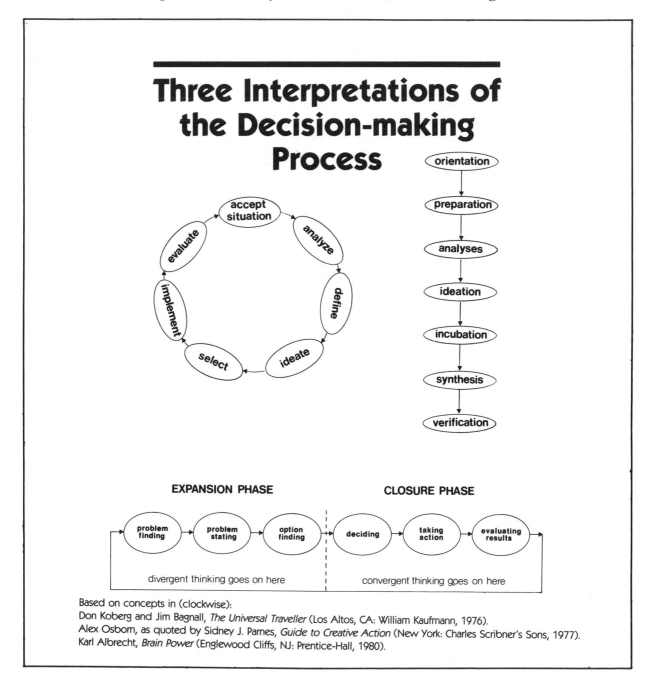

Three Interpretations of the Decision-making Process

accept situation → analyze → define → ideate → select → implement → evaluate

orientation → preparation → analyses → ideation → incubation → synthesis → verification

EXPANSION PHASE

CLOSURE PHASE

problem finding → problem stating → option finding → deciding → taking action → evaluating results

divergent thinking goes on here | convergent thinking goes on here

Based on concepts in (clockwise):
Don Koberg and Jim Bagnall, *The Universal Traveller* (Los Altos, CA: William Kaufmann, 1976).
Alex Osborn, as quoted by Sidney J. Parnes, *Guide to Creative Action* (New York: Charles Scribner's Sons, 1977).
Karl Albrecht, *Brain Power* (Englewood Cliffs, NJ: Prentice-Hall, 1980).

Psych-up

Hindsight

We learn by experience. We seek pleasure and avoid pain according to what has given us pleasure and pain in the past. If we repeat a particular type of experience again and again, we will inevitably learn more about that experience. If we wish to acquire knowledge or master a task in a certain area, we can train ourselves over time.

The experiences that impress us the most are those that result from our conscious decisions. The facts we remember the most vividly from school are those we were told when we raised our hands and asked questions. The developments in our jobs from which we derive the most education are those we personally set in motion. The lessons we learn the best from relationships are those we teach ourselves.

How much we actually learn from our decision-making experiences depends on how much we pay attention to our decisions when we make them and, most critically, on how much we review past decisions whenever we are faced with a new decision of the same nature. The more attention paid and the more review conducted, the more we grow.

Consider each of the following categories of experience in your life. For each category, think of some decisions you have made and applied in the past. Answer the questions posed in each category to the best of your ability.

Work

1. What is one of the most successful decisions I ever made?

_____

_____

_____

2. What, specifically, made it so successful?

_____

_____

_____

3. What were the factors involved in reaching that decision?

_____

_____

4. What is one of the worst decisions I ever made?

_____

_____

_____

5. What, specifically, made it so bad?

_____

_____

_____

6. What were the factors involved in reaching that decision?

_____

_____

_____

Leisure

1. What is one of the easiest decisions I have ever made?

_____

_____

_____

2. What, specifically, made it so easy?

_____

_____

_____

3. What were the factors involved in reaching that decision?

_____

_____

4. What is one of the most difficult decisions I ever made?

5. What, specifically, made it so difficult?

6. What were the factors involved in reaching that decision?

Possessions

1. What is one of the most unusual decisions I ever made?

2. What, specifically, made it so unusual?

3. What were the factors involved in reaching that decision?

_____

_____

_____

4. What is one kind of decision that I repeatedly face?

_____

_____

_____

5. What, in specific cases, have been the results of this kind of decision?

_____

_____

_____

6. What factors vary from case to case when I am faced with this kind of decision?

_____

_____

_____

Who are you? How would you describe your life to a reporter?

Behavioral scientists tell us that our first impulse in responding to such questions is to define ourselves in terms of how we feel others see us or in terms of how we feel the outside world has influenced our personal development. But taking inventory of our decisions—the choices we have made, how and why we have made them, and the results of those choices—is the only way to examine the shape that we ourselves have given to our lives. Only by interpreting our experience this way can we learn what we need to know to develop strategies for improving our lives.

Suppose you answered the question "What is one of the most successful decisions I ever made?" under the category "Work" as "deciding to request more authority in dealing with clients." What made that decision so successful could have been any one, or all, of the following results—some of which you may not have foreseen:

- enjoying more satisfactory interactions with clients
- increasing the scope of negotiations with clients
- making business with clients more efficient
- making business with clients more profitable
- learning more about clients' needs, concerns, and interests

Before you made the decision, you may have considered:

- how prepared you were to devote more time and energy to your business
- how your family, friends, coworkers, and boss would feel about your having more power
- the mood of your boss at the time
- how the business was doing at the time
- the extent to which you felt mentally and physically equipped to assume new authority
- specific exchanges with clients that revealed problems and opportunities you might face with new authority
- the desire to revive a flagging interest in your job
- the desire to compete with others
- the desire to qualify eventually for increased pay or benefits or a promotion
- a magazine article you read on the bus one morning
- an idea an acquaintance put into your head
- the words of a high school coach
- your surge of confidence after losing twenty-five pounds

As you examine your responses to the psych-up questions, consider these issues:

1. Can I see any pattern (or patterns) in the way I make decisions?

2. What if things had been different?
   - How might a successful decision have failed?
   - How might a decision that was a failure have succeeded?
   - How might an easy decision have been more difficult to make?
   - How might a difficult decision have been more easily made?
   - If it was an unusual decision, under what circumstances would I make the same type of decision again?

- If it was a typical, routine kind of decision, how could I make the decision more challenging and more potentially rewarding?

3. How can I improve the way I make decisions?

More Psych-ups

- Think of other decisions you have made in each category.

- Switch the questions under each category. For example, consider the category "Work" and ask yourself the questions under the category "Possessions."

- Think of other categories of experiences and ask yourself the same questions. Here are some additional categories to get you started: education, health, friendship, love, sex, morals. You can also break down such general categories into more specific ones.

- Draw up a history of a specific decision you have made. Arrange in chronological order all the circumstances relating to your reaching that decision, then implementing that decision and, finally, living with the results.

Exercise 1

Win, Place, and Show: Making Choices

Anyone who bets on a filly named Peachy Melba to win a horse race because his or her mother's name is Melba knows how arbitrarily one can summon up complete faith in a necessarily spur-of-the-moment decision.

The more objective information one brings to bear on a decision, the better the chances are that the decision will be good. Timing, however, can play a strong role in decision-making. In many situations, particularly ones that we do not initiate, there simply is not enough time to evaluate all the data before the moment for action.

While it is never wise in real life to force ourselves to make a decision if no time pressure exists, and if we have not thoroughly examined the decision environment, it is wise to do so as a mental exercise. It sharpens our ability to think on our feet and reveals all sorts of unconscious, semiconscious, and conscious preferences and predispositions that may be deciding factors in many of the decisions we make, however much time and information we have.

Each of the following examples presents you with three options. Consider each group briefly and then arrange the options according to your first, second, and third choices. Do not add qualifiers to your choices ("I would do this if . . .") or create ties between or among the options. After you have made your decisions, briefly explain why you made them.

EXAMPLE:

I am marooned on a small island for three months. I have sufficent food, drink, clothing, and shelter, and I am offered the following entertainment options:

a. a giant-screen state-of-the-art television capable of receiving all the programs I could watch at home

b. a large library of books, representing a wide range of fiction, nonfiction, poetry, drama, and reference works

c. a complete state-of-the-art stereo system and a huge set of records and tapes

first choice: b
second choice: a
third choice: c

why?:   I love to read, and I'd probably get more day-to-day variety from books, given my reading habits as opposed to my viewing and listening habits. I prefer television to records and tapes in this situation because I would probably want to keep some sort of contact with the outside world.

1. I have to discuss a sensitive personal issue with a close friend. I have the following options about where to meet this friend:

a. my place

b. my friend's place

c. some other place

first choice:
second choice:
third choice:

why?: _____

_____

_____

_____

2. I am completely redecorating and refurnishing my living room. I am offered the following main color options:

a. red

b. blue

c. brown

first choice:
second choice:
third choice:

why?: _____

_____

_____

_____

3. I can go on vacation for a month. I can choose to go to:

a. *Italy*

b. *the United Kingdom*

c. *Japan*

first choice:
second choice:
third choice:

why?: _____

_____

_____

_____

4. I have an opportunity to form a close friendship with someone. I have the following options regarding the profession of this person:

a. painter

b. writer

c. actor

first choice:
second choice:
third choice:

why?: _____

_____

_____

_____

5. I have a dog. I am offered the following options for the name of this dog:

a. Moonie

b. Underfoot

c. Shazzam

first choice:
second choice:
third choice:

why?: _____

_____

_____

_____

6. I can change an aspect of my body. I have the following options regarding what to change:

a. my hair

b. my face

c. my body shape

first choice:
second choice:
third choice:

why?: _____

_____

_____

_____

_____

_____

More Workouts

• Perform this same exercise, focusing on any subject that includes or suggests a lot of alternatives and selecting three of them at random. Here are some suggestions to get you started:

1. Look at a map and, closing your eyes, lightly touch three different spots with a pencil (if you land in a body of water, imagine you are at the nearest spot of land). Assume you could visit these places, and rate them accordingly.
2. Take a phone book and, closing your eyes and choosing three pages at random, pick three different names. Imagine you had these options for your own new name and rate them accordingly.
3. Take any catalogue of merchandise and, closing your eyes, choose three pages at random and pick three different items. Assume you could have these items and rate them accordingly.

• Imagine you find a magic lamp and rub it. A genie appears to grant you three wishes regarding one particular aspect of your life—work, leisure, health, relationships, education, whatever. The wishes have to be specific. In other words, an individual wish cannot include such general words as *every, all,* or *best possible,* and it cannot contain subparts. What would those three wishes be? Why? Which would you choose and why if the genie said that you could only have two of your wishes? One of your wishes?

"When choosing between two evils, I always like to take the one I've never tried before."—Mae West

Exercise 2

The Journey Versus the Step: Establishing Goals

Scholars debate whether Confucius or Lao-tzu first said, "A journey of a thousand miles must begin with a single step," but we are all familiar with the adage. Our culture tends to be action-oriented, and so it is the "single step" part that gets most of our attention. We often forget that our conception of the overall journey determines how, where, why, and when we make the first step.

Many people confuse activities with goals. A goal is what we want to achieve as a result of one or more activities—for example, "to have a personal income of $50,000 by this time next year." An activity is what we do to accomplish a goal—for example, "sell fifty pots this month." When a friend says he or she wants to quit smoking, he or she is talking about an activity (grinding a butt into an ashtray), not a goal. Our friend's actual goal is something like "to achieve complete independence from the habit of smoking by next week," which could involve a wide range of goal-directed activities.

To be effective, a goal needs to be specific, measurable, and related to time so we know where and how we are going and so we can assess our progress along the way. Some goals are by their very nature more specific and measurable than others, especially goals that deal with items that can be easily quantified, like money or production units. But even when we are dealing with intangibles like intelligence, beauty, or assertiveness, we can make our goal more specific and measurable (and therefore more conceivable and motivating) by describing those otherwise vague qualities as precisely as we can. Ask yourself, for example, "What do I want my intelligence to be capable of doing?" "Is there a way I can 'rate' its performance?" "What do I want to look like?" "Is there a picture I could draw or a person I could use as a model?" "What do I hope to gain by being assertive?" "How would I define the degree of assertiveness I want?"

Consider each of the activities below. For each activity, state a goal to which it could relate. In each goal statement, express the desired result as specifically as possible, develop criteria by which progress toward that result can be measured, and include an appropriate deadline. You may find it helpful to begin each goal statement with the phrase to achieve *or* to have *or* to realize, *so that you will not wind up with another version of an activity statement instead of a goal statement.*

EXAMPLE:

Playing racquetball:

goal statement: To achieve a comprehensive mastery of the sport of racquetball sufficient enough to qualify me for inclusion in the A-level competition at the Acme Racquetball Club by March 1.

1. Losing weight:

goal statement:

_____

_____

2. Attending a class on career development:

goal statement:

_____

_____

_____

3. Buying a new kitchen table:

goal statement:

_____

_____

_____

4. Reading a nonfiction book:

goal statement:

_____

_____

_____

5. Planting a garden:

goal statement:

_____

_____

_____

6. Changing jobs:

goal statement:

_____

_____

More Workouts

• Repeat the exercise, thinking up alternative goals that fit the same activities.

• Choose any activity and think up appropriate goals. As you develop proficiency, focus more and more on activities that are a part of your own life and formulate goals that are realistic but will stretch your capabilities.

• Confusing an activity with a goal is so easy and common that we can spot evidence of it every day if we make an effort. Take note during one day of all the times you hear or read a goal statement that is, in fact, the statement of an activity. Then take some of these activity statements and turn them into effective goal statements.

Exercise 3

Out of the Armchair: Moving Toward Your Goals

Sitting back in a comfortable chair and entertaining yourself with visions and descriptions of who you would like to be, what you would like to accomplish, and where you would like to go can be one of the most exciting and rewarding of all mental exercises. But once you manage to fashion a particular goal, sooner or later you need to plan to achieve it and act on your plan. If you fail to do this, you will not only never be who you would like to be, accomplish what you want to accomplish, or go where you would like to be, you will also wreck your capability to derive pleasure from your daydreams. They will turn into nightmarish reminders of an ongoing conflict between two decisions you have made: the consciously generated yes to your goals and the subconsciously generated no to doing anything about them.

Committing yourself to a goal begins with planning the activities you will perform to achieve that goal. The more detailed your plan, the better you will know where you are going and the easier it will be to get there.

For each of the goals listed below, state several activities that could be performed to achieve that goal. Be as specific and as imaginative as you wish.

Goal: to realize a circulation increase of 100,000 for the *West Jefferson Daily Dispatch* in four months

EXAMPLE:

Activities:

• develop and run an exciting four-month contest

• conduct a subscription drive over four months

• double the number of stands selling the paper over the next couple of weeks.

• find and print a sensational human-interest story as soon as possible and follow up with other equally sensational stories

• conduct a public survey over the next week to find out what people want in a newspaper

• conduct a private survey among newspaper staff members over the next week to generate ideas for improving circulation

1. *Goal:* to achieve a knowledge and understanding of the major classical composers by the end of the summer so that I can enjoy the next concert season

Activities:

_____

_____

_____

_____

_____

2. *Goal:* to have one more free hour every day by next week

Activities:

_____

_____

_____

_____

_____

3. *Goal:* to possess a burnt-sienna Cadillac convertible by June 1

Activities:

_____

_____

_____

_____

_____

4. *Goal:* to achieve the capability of running 5 miles in 8 minutes in 6 months' time

Activities:

_____

_____

_____

_____

_____

_____

5. *Goal:* To have a regularly scheduled weekly card game with the same group of people by the end of the month

Activities:

_____

_____

_____

_____

_____

_____

_____

More Workouts

• Perform this same exercise using any goals. It will be especially useful if you formulate goals based on your own desires, needs, and concerns.

• Focus on a single goal and create a specific action plan. To do this, apply the following steps to create a written record:

1. List all the activities you can that would help to achieve the goal.

2. Break down each activity into components.

3. Determine a logical sequence for performing these tasks.

4. Estimate the time it will take to perform each one.

5. Identify the resources required to accomplish each task in the time required.

6. Review the entire plan and develop contingency plans for any constraints, obstacles, or opportunities that may occur.

Exercise 4

Operation Red Flag: Making Decisions in a Crisis

Our most memorable decisions are often those we make in emergencies, when our adrenaline is up and all our faculties are quickly brought to attention. Circumstances suddenly threaten to take over unless we have the power and agility to respond to the change in such a manner that we can continue to serve our objectives.

How effectively we execute an operation red flag depends on how well we have developed our general decision-making skills. The more consistently we keep our goals in mind and the more thoughtfully we plan to achieve them, the more prepared we will be to handle crises effectively. When unusual situations arise, we have simply to rethink our strategy rather than to think from scratch. We can say, "How shall I *manage* this situation, given my objectives and plans?" rather than, "What shall I *do* now?" The more effectively we have planned in advance to achieve goals, the more likely it is that we have already anticipated possible crises and have contingency plans.

The process of handling an operation red flag if you do not have a preconceived contingency plan is the same as the process for handling any decision—only the time you have for the process is compressed. First, ask yourself, "What is the overall goal relative to this situation? What do I want to have happen as the result of any activity I wind up performing?" Then, ask yourself, "What are all the possible action alternatives that would help me achieve this goal?" Finally, ask yourself, "What action is most likely to further progress to the goal, given the circumstances?"

Assume you are faced with each of the crisis situations listed below. For each situation, ask yourself, "What is the overall goal?" Consider all possible alternatives for action and then state both what you would do to help achieve that goal, given the circumstances ("Action"), and how you might have planned in advance to prepare for this type of emergency ("Advance planning").

EXAMPLE:

You are scheduled to address several of your coworkers and bosses regarding a major new business idea you have at an early morning meeting. Your alarm fails to function that morning, and you wake up too late to make it to work in time for the meeting. You also discover that you cannot locate your notes; you are fairly certain you brought them home with you, and you are not sure where they could be if you left them in your office. What do you decide to do?

Action: Call my immediate superior, state that I am unable to make the meeting, and request my superior's assistance in rescheduling the meeting for the following day, which will give me time to track down or re-create my notes. If this is not possible, explain the idea to my superior so that my superior can conduct the meeting in my absence, for the purpose of eliciting initial reactions to the idea to which I can respond at a later meeting. If this is not possible, explain the idea to one of my coworkers so that he or she can conduct the meeting.

Advance planning:

• Make three copies of my notes and keep one copy in a definite location at work, use one copy as a working copy, and keep one copy in a definite location at home.

• Have a back-up alarm.

• Keep my superior or a trusted coworker regularly informed (and motivated) about my ideas.

• Try to avoid scheduling such a meeting early in the morning so that I can have office time during the day before the meeting.

1. You are traveling by train to a city two hours away to keep a 10:00 A.M. appointment with a medical specialist. After the appointment, you go to the train station to catch the noon train home. The train is canceled and you cannot get home any other way before 6:00 P.M., when the next train leaves. You have $5 (no credit cards) for all expenses other than your train fare. How do you spend your day in the city?

Action:

_____

_____

_____

_____

_____

Advance planning:

_____

_____

_____

_____

2. You live in a small town and are chairperson of the committee to paint the town meeting hall in time for the Fourth of July celebration. You are working with a very limited budget, so you have asked for volunteers. A number of townspeople have agreed to help paint the meeting house during their spare time. Weeks go by, the Fourth of July is fast approaching, and little or nothing has been done. What do you decide to do?

Action:

_____

_____

_____

_____

Advance planning:

_____

_____

_____

3. Your lover or spouse tells you that he or she is in love with someone else, insisting that he or she still loves you, did not choose to fall in love with the other person, and did not turn to that person because of any dissatisfaction with you. What do you decide to do?

Action:

_____

_____

_____

_____

Advance planning:

_____

_____

_____

4. You are a warden at an island prison. Just offshore is a string of buoys surrounding the island, with signs warning all boats to keep away. Nevertheless, pleasure craft and city sightseeing boats continually circle the island and occasionally come too near. The tower guards, bored with the monotony of their job, take advantage of such opportunities to fire warning shots into the water, which they are empowered to do. Lately, this has resulted in angry letters to newspaper editors and complaints from city legislators. Your superior has demanded that you make a decision right away. What do you decide to do?

Action:

_____

_____

_____

_____

Advance planning:

_____

_____

_____

_____

More Workouts

• Perform this same exercise with any crisis about which you read or hear or any crisis you can anticipate happening in your life.

• Perform this same exercise with any situation you can think up that is sudden but not necessarily a crisis. Be as imaginative as possible, and consider not only ways to handle the situation but also ways to profit from it. Here are some examples to get you started:

1. You are suddenly left alone for an afternoon with a six-year-old child you do not know well.

2. You are suddenly laid off for six months with full pay.

3. You suddenly receive a $500 gift certificate at a major pet store that must be spent within a week.

4. You suddenly find yourself alone in a waiting room with a famous person you greatly admire whom you have never met before.

"Life is the art of drawing sufficient conclusions from insufficient premises."
—Samuel Butler

Mind Play

• Role-playing—assuming a role that you do not in fact have, or enacting someone else's role—compels you to understand and anticipate the decisions of other people both rationally and emotionally. You can try role-playing by creating scripts between two characters in a hypothetical situation. Choose a decision-making issue involving two different points of view, and either develop a confrontational dialogue in your head or speak it out loud or, best of all, jot it down on paper. Try to be as objective as possible in your dialogue, and assume each character's role in turn. Here are some samples to get you started:

a. You meet with your boss to ask for a raise.

b. Your boss meets with you to praise or condemn your work.

c. You try to win over an enemy.

d. A friend accuses you of being racist.

e. You are a single member of the opposite sex trying to discourage a friend's persistent efforts to begin a romance with you.

f. You are a college student and receive a grade you think is unfair. If it were changed to the grade you think you deserve, you would make the academic honor list. Your teacher seems to be a reasonable, if strict, person, so you meet with her, determined to convince her to change the grade.

g. A very dear friend of yours has been staying with you and your spouse for several days. Although you have enjoyed the visit, your spouse has not and insists that you ask the friend to leave. You understand your spouse's point of view and agree to do this. You meet with the friend.

You can also role-play with friends. In advance, think up confrontations that are either classic (the teenage boy trying to convince his girl friend's father to let him marry his daughter) or amusingly unusual (a stranger at the door who must get you to say "I want to rub a grapefruit in your face" to win a bet). Then write down each character's basic description and goal on a separate piece of paper, to be drawn as lots by the two players. Do not let either of the two players know the other person's description and goal ahead of time.

• Play decision-making games with objects around you. Imagine you had to give away all your possessions today. To whom would you give what? Why? Imagine you had five minutes to get stuff outside your door before everything disappeared. What would you choose? Why?

• Take a particular area of life—work, leisure, relationships, possessions, whatever—and review all the decisions you have made and experiences you have had relating to this area. Then make up your own "wise sayings"—maxims, adages, or proverbs that you can consider when making future decisions of the same kind. Your wise sayings can range from the highly practical and prosaic (for example, "Never venture outside without a pencil and paper") to the whimsical and poetic (for example, "No doubts, go ahead; many doubts, stay in bed").

More Decision-making Exercises

• Goals can be translated into higher goals (supergoals) or lower goals (subgoals). For example, you may form the goal "to have achieved the title of general manager by two years from now." A supergoal may be "to have achieved the title of executive vice-president by six years from now." A subgoal may be "to have achieved the title of director by one year from now." Practice translating individual personal goals into supergoals and subgoals.

• "Everybody has some opinion about everything," according to Ann Landers. Usually, however, our opinions are relatively undeveloped—just enough to spark conversation at a party or give us our bearings when we are confronted with a controversy. Choose one of your opinions (for example, about criminal justice, an international conflict, child rearing, or sports statistics) and develop goals relating to that opinion: Ask yourself, for example, "What's wrong with this situation?" "What results would I like to see happen?" Then outline activities that would help achieve those goals. Putting your opinions through this decision-making process will refine them and give them more power.

• A well-organized daily "to do" list helps you manage your time effectively by equipping you to make the decisions each day that are the most appropriate for achieving the goals you want to achieve. Create such a list for each day, following these steps:

1. Every evening, or the first thing the next morning, write down all the activities you want to perform or need to perform the following day.

2. Relate each of the activities to a goal (what you want to achieve as a result of that activity). Indicate each goal beside the corresponding activity.

3. Consider whether each goal represents a result you really want to achieve and whether each activity represents a good way to achieve its goal. Modify your goals and/or activities accordingly.

4. For each activity-plus-goal, ask yourself these questions:

   a. Do I need to do the activity today to stand the best chance of achieving my goal? If the answer is yes, mark it A. If not, mark it B. Be sure to consider the possibility of breaking down an activity into separate tasks before making any final judgments.

   b. How important is this particular goal compared to the other goals? If it is one of your more important goals, put a plus sign next to the A or B. If it is one of your less important goals, put a minus sign next to the A or B.

5. Organize your final "to do" list according to your priority activities and goals: A+ items first, then A− items, then B+ items, and finally, B− items. Include an estimate of how much time each activity might take.

• Daily scheduling decisions are among the most difficult decisions, since so many factors have to be anticipated. At what time you perform different activities depends on how much control you have over what happens that day, your mood, and how easily you are able to accomplish the tasks. Using a daily "to do" list, decide upon a daily schedule in advance, based on the following considerations:

1. Distinguish between "initiated" items (those whose scheduling is in your control) and "response" items (those whose scheduling is outside your control, including both prescheduled

events and possible interruptions). Try to establish or anticipate the time periods when you need to be (or are willing to be) subject to response items, and schedule initiated items so that they will not conflict with these time periods.

2. Examine your own needs and work patterns to determine the best time to perform different types of activities. Ask yourself, for example, "When during the average day do I most successfully manage activities that require deep thought?" Try to allocate this time for your most challenging activities.

3. Consolidate similar activities (for example, all your phone calls, all your household maintenance tasks, all your writing tasks) and schedule them in single blocks of time that are best suited for accomplishing them.

• Once you have decided upon a course of action based on a predetermined goal, you are ready to consider giving yourself an added incentive for reaching that goal. Think up possible rewards that are appropriate for achieving different goals. Consider also the goals of other people who play a part in achieving your own goals. What incentives could you offer them?

• Consider separate goals and action plans you have developed—either hypothetical ones you have invented for mental exercise or actual ones. Think of all the ways you might monitor progress toward a particular goal.

• Keep a journal of all the decisions you make each day or each week. Note also the ongoing results of previous decisions and new issues that crop up that seem to invite decision-making.

Creativity Workouts

While conducting research for *What Does Childhood Taste Like?* I accumulated almost one hundred definitions of creativity. Over half of them hinge on an analogy to birth.

"Creative ideas seem to spring forth from the unknown, like the first wail of a newborn infant," wrote Voltaire. It certainly does *seem* this way. Just as no one can explain what causes a human being to come to life, no one can explain what causes a creative idea to occur in our minds. Genetic material somehow combines to form a human being, given chance and the right circumstances. Impression-laden thoughts somehow combine to form a creative idea, given chance and the right circumstances.

Although there is no formula we can devise for producing a new life or a creative idea, there is much we can do in both cases to provide the right circumstances for conception and to tend and develop the product of that conception. Both require a certain degree of knowledge, a certain degree of cooperation with our instincts and, yes, a certain degree of passion.

The first step in preparing to be creative is to understand what constitutes a creative idea. A creative idea is not necessarily an idea that no one has ever had before; nor does being creative mean being artistic or intelligent. A creative idea is one that seems unusually fresh because we witness it taking shape in our own minds—alongside, but separate from, ideas that we mechanically construct simply by arranging data and deriving conclusions. Being creative means being the generator of our own ideas—letting them originate within our minds rather than borrowing them from other sources.

A creative idea possesses a quality of independence, as does the result of such an idea, whether it be a painting, a football strategy, or an omelet. Cognitive scientists may not be able to define what a creative idea is, but we all know one when it happens: We can feel it. According to Dr. Philip Moss, a consultant in creative thinking whose clients include General Electric, Mobil Oil, and the U.S. Army, "The mind has an almost physical reaction to a creative thought." To Archimedes, the ancient Greek philosopher who was suddenly struck by a new theory of hydraulics while taking a bath, this reaction was the "eureka!" experience. To Martin Gardner, the American mathematician and puzzle creator, this reaction is the "aha!" or "gotcha!" experience.

In keeping with the birth image for a creative idea, the archetypal image for the creative person is the infant. In early childhood, we were all highly creative. We had to be to get rolling in life. Charged with the energy of our own birth and untamed by adult-world mental programming, we remained completely open-minded, conscious witnesses of the birth of every "new" idea in our heads, enabling us rapidly to become individuals in our own right.

Only years of postchildhood conformity—caused by yielding to habits, fears, and the massive authority of preestablished, logical ways of perceiving and doing things—prevents us from being as attuned to our creative ideas as we once were. Therefore, most suggestions for enhancing personal creativity involve deliberately pursuing unhabitual, nongoal-oriented, and atypical mental activities with as much confidence and sense of play as we can. It is impossible for us to escape altogether our "adult" mentality—which urges us to be serious and rational—but we can develop a highly effective "child" mentality to be its inspirational partner.

Most experts on the subject of creativity building advocate a threefold program, which can be summarized as follows:

1. *Break your routine.* We have all had the experience of stewing over a problem or opportunity for hours at a time, only to sit back and relax afterward and have a solution pop into our heads. The subconscious mind needs a chance to process the concerns of the conscious mind, uninhibited by logic or preoccupation with details and consequences. Students cramming for an examination are advised to go out and see a movie the night before the examination precisely so that they have this unconscious processing time. If our conscious minds are suffering an energy lag regarding a certain subject, it is wise to shift gears and return to the subject later, with a fresh point of view.

2. *Make your luck work for you.* Inspiration frequently comes by accident, and because we do not plan for an accident, we tend to disregard whatever vision of opportunity the accident may provide. Creative genius is often a matter of seizing upon happy accidents of thought and turning them to account. Sir Isaac Newton did this when he was hit on the head by an apple falling from a tree. He developed an entirely new theory about gravity. Duke Ellington did this when he was conducting an outdoor concert and a noisy plane appeared above the orchestra. He changed the tempo of the piece the orchestra was playing to incorporate the sounds that the plane was making. Ivory soap, "the soap that floats," was discovered by someone who inadvertently let the machine that stirred the soap run for a longer than usual time period. Such moments are called moments of *serendipity,* a word coined from Horace Walpole's story of the princes of Serendip, who were continually making discoveries of things they were not looking for while they were looking for something else.

3. *Regularly perform independent mental activities designed to encourage creativity.* Cognitive science has produced and tested many exercises that we can use to develop our creative powers. "Just as we can throttle our imagination," notes Alex F. Osborn, a pioneer in the field of creativity enhancement, "we can likewise accelerate it. As in any other art, individual creativity can be implemented by certain 'techniques.'" The best and most comprehensive of these techniques have been assimilated into this program.

The exercises in this chapter will help you to gain a new spirit of exploration and adventure in your mental life, to increase your capacity for generating, recognizing, and developing creative ideas, and to transcend the limitations of conventional approaches to problem-solving, opportunity detection, and decision-making.

Psych-up

Riddling

While searching for his identity, Oedipus came to a crossroads guarded by a sphinx. "To pass by me," said the sphinx, "you must solve my riddle. If you fail to solve it, you die. The riddle is: What walks on four legs in the morning, two legs at noon, and three legs in the evening?" "Man," Oedipus answered, "for he crawls in the morning of his life, stands on his own two feet at the noontime of his life, and moves with the aid of a cane in the evening of his life."

Oedipus passed.

Solving a riddle is an especially challenging and imaginative workout for our analytical minds. Making up a riddle, or riddling, exercises our creative minds by forcing them to envision the ordinary in fresh and original ways.

Children love riddles because they make fun out of a process that is their primary work: looking at the world around them for the first time and defining items to fit their personal sense of reality. Their definitions do not need to be rational or comprehensive to work. A child cannot be expected to be rational; but we can count on a child to learn and to grow and to become wise, regardless. "What has a stone on its head and a finger in its mouth?" goes one popular children's riddle. The answer? A ring. "What's deaf, dumb, and blind, and always tells the truth?" A mirror. On a less sophisticated level, a child sees a horse as a chair that has a face and moves around or an ice-cream cone as two circles that melt into a triangle or Grandfather as a cross between Santa Claus and the bogeyman.

Practice riddling by offering creative definitions for each of the items listed below. Your definitions do not have to be especially clever. They simply need to cast an imaginative light on what to the rational mind seems perfectly, and banally, obvious.

1. Ball-point pen _____

_____

_____

2. Clam _____

_____

_____

3. Streetlight _____

4. Bathtub _____

_____

_____

5. Giraffe _____

_____

_____

6. Camera _____

_____

_____

7. Motel _____

_____

_____

8. Dinosaur _____

_____

_____

9. Board of directors _____

_____

_____

10. Brain surgeon _____

_____

_____

Riddles tease us and force us beyond the boundaries of linear thinking, where we experience all sorts of novel impressions. Puns and jokes do the same thing.

Our reaction to riddles, puns, and jokes—internal laughter—is much like the sensation triggered by any creative idea. "Laughter," according to Freud, "is economy in the expenditure of emotion." In other words, we are surprised by feelings that we do not know how to release in a rational or efficient manner.

Riddling is a way of setting up that surprise and prompting the inner laughter that tells us we have broken through our logical, systematic way of perceiving things. Riddling also spurs our creativity in other ways:

• It enables us to "re-create" a whole through randomly combining some of its parts, so that the potential of the whole, rather than its actuality, becomes more evident. When we say, "A pencil is a stick that talks as it walks," for example, we see the pencil's dynamics and possibilities far more than if we consider it analytically as "an implement for writing, drawing, or notating consisting of a small cylinder of a solid marking substance typically enclosed by wood." If we say that "a cold is something we can give away and still keep," we automatically form conceptions of disease and intimacy that are not at all inspired by the clinical point of view that a cold is "a communicable body disorder popularly associated with respiratory discomfort and chilling."

• It confronts us with the special meaning that things have for us, a meaning that does not often emerge if we just look at something objectively. For example, by describing a squirrel as "part rat, part wolf, and part nuts," it emerges as a symbol of something irrational and menacing.

• It provides us with a means of accepting and expressing the mysterious. A five-year-old friend of mine who cannot yet understand a computer is well on her way when she defines it temporarily as "a television that turns you on." We may not be able to fathom quantum physics, but we get a start by imagining light that cannot be seen and sound that cannot be heard.

Examine the riddles you have created and ask yourself these questions: "What puzzles me, or what seems odd, about the subject of the riddle?" "What attitude does the riddle reveal about that subject?" "What other possible answers—even fanciful ones—could I give that would satisfy the conditions set up by the riddle?" "What other riddles could I create using the same subject?" "What ideas does the riddle inspire?"

More Psych-ups

• Concentrate on one type of riddle, using whatever subject (or subjects) you wish. Types of riddles include:

1. Riddles beginning with "what" that refer to an item existing in either the real world or an

imaginary world (such as, "What has a neck and no head, two arms and no hands?" A shirt. "What goes z-z-z-b, z-z-z-b?" A bee flying backward.)

2. Riddles beginning with "why" or "what would happen if" that have a gag answer (such as, "Why does an elephant wear green shoes?" So no one will notice him when he tiptoes across a pool table. "What would happen if a bird got run over by a lawn mower?" Shredded tweet.)

3. Riddles based on imaginary conversations (such as, "What did the drop of ink say to the paper?" My mother is in the pen and I don't know how long the sentence will be. "What did one eye say to the other eye?" Something smells between us.)

4. Riddles based on "crisscrossing" (such as, "What do you get when you cross a duck and a cow?" Quackers and milk.)

5. Riddles based on similarities or differences (such as, "Why is a palm tree like a calendar?" Both give dates. "What's the difference between a match and a cat?" The match lights on its head and the cat lights on its feet.)

• Choose one subject and generate as many different riddles as you can based on that subject, using the above list of riddle types as a guide.

Exercise 1

Presto!: Imagining Things Are Different

The creative person is a magician—someone who appears to have a mystical inner power for causing one thing to change into another thing altogether. In fact, we all possess this power, whether we choose to use it or not. The mind can imaginatively transform anything it perceives by rearranging its aspects, by emphasizing some aspects and downplaying others, or by altering some aspects so that the thing itself takes on an entirely different character.

Most of the time we suppress this type of mental activity, either consciously or unconsciously, because there is no reason for it. In most day-to-day situations, there is even a strong reason against it: It can distract us from what we know to be "real" and confuse us by producing a host of images that contradict one another. But as a tool for creativity, this power needs to be channeled and developed by regular exercise so that we can use it to see beyond what merely *is* to what *might be.*

Three possible changes are listed for each of the items below. Consider each change individually and identify possible uses and/or advantages of the changed item. Be as fanciful or as practical as you wish. Also feel free in each case to make any additional changes, as long as you include the one that is signified.

EXAMPLE:

Vacuum cleaner:

with the action reversed: could be used to dry things (for example, paint, hair, water spots on walls and fabric); could be used to blow things off surfaces (for example, sawdust from wood, sand or snow from pathways and steps)

made completely transparent: could see when the bag was full and where any problem was in the motor

with the action made stronger: would pick up especially tenacious items, like animal hair and paper scraps, more effectively; with a wider mouth could be used to pick up heavier trash items, peel paint, pull apart items that are stuck together

1. Tennis shoe:

made larger:

_____

_____

_____

made smaller:

_____
_____
_____

with a removable sole:

_____
_____
_____

2. Kitchen stove:

with the action reversed:

_____
_____
_____

with detachable components:

_____
_____
_____

that glowed in the dark:

_____
_____
_____

3. Straightback chair without arms:

made larger:

_____

_____

_____

made transparent:

_____

_____

_____

given an assortment of legs:

_____

_____

_____

4. Ceiling:
made reflective:

_____

_____

that could be raised and lowered:

_____

_____

_____

that could be rolled back, revealing the sky:

_____

_____

_____

"Nothing comes from doing nothing."—Shakespeare

More Workouts

• Each exercise session, pick a different area of experience—work, leisure, health, relationships, possessions, whatever—and imagine how you would change things if you were a magician. Consider not only practical changes but also fantasy changes. Be sure to focus on items that already exist and work toward change; in other words, do not just eliminate items altogether and replace them with entirely different items.

• In his seminal book on creativity, *Applied Imagination,* Alex F. Osborn offers a series of basic questions that can trigger insights into how any subject may be changed. Choose a particular object, idea, situation, or process and consider it in the light of these questions (some may not be appropriate):

1. Can it be put to other uses? (Are there new ways to use it as it is? Are there other uses if it is modified?)

2. Can it be adapted? (What else is like this? What other ideas does it suggest?)

3. Can it be modified? (Can the meaning, color, motion, sound, odor, taste, form, or shape be changed? Are there other changes that can be made?)

4. Can it be magnified? (What to add? Greater frequency? Stronger? Larger? Plus ingredient? Multiply?)

5. Can it be minified? (What to subtract? Eliminate? Smaller? Lighter? Slower? Split up? Less frequent?)

6. Can it be substituted? (What else instead? Other place? Other time?)

7. Can it be rearranged? (Other layout? Other sequence? Change of pace?)

8. Can it be reversed? (Opposites? Turn it backward? Turn it upside down? Turn it inside out?)

9. Can it be combined? (How about a blend, an assortment? Combine purposes? Combine ideas?)

Exercise 2

What If: Forcing Associations to Trigger New Ideas

Everything that is creative has a quality of strangeness to it. This strangeness cannot be separated from what gives a creative idea or product its overall independent nature. For this reason, cognitive scientists and creativity experts recommend randomly pairing two items and mentally forcing links between them. This gives the mind practice in confronting what is strange and rendering it intelligible.

One dimension of being creative is the ability to make the ordinary seem newly mysterious. The corresponding dimension that makes creativity a dynamic process is the capacity to make the mysterious seem ordinary. In this respect, the creator is a true poet. The very word *poet*, in fact, comes from the Greek word for creator.

Randomly choose three pairs of terms, each containing one of the numbered adjectives and one of the lettered nouns in the columns below. Before you look at the columns closely, you may want to choose pairs in advance by selecting three numbers from 1 through 8 and three letters from "a" through "h" and putting them in three pairs now. Or else you can close your eyes and stab at the page until you have created three pairs. Once you have three pairs, imagine that each phrase you have made is the name of a new product you are marketing for the general consumer. For each product, offer a brief description of its features and benefits.

EXAMPLE:

Product name: elastic bureau

> *features:* a lightweight chest of four drawers made of strong but soft rubber that hangs from a collapsible thin stainless-steel frame; each drawer expands to fit the material put inside it

> *benefits:*
> takes up only as much space as you need or want it to; easy to pack; convenient for home use, office use, travel use, and camp use (can be left outdoors): won't rust or chip

Adjectives	*Nouns*
1. space-age	a. bed
2. traveling	b. table
3. emergency	c. banana
4. musical	d. plant
5. mind-bending	e. rug
6. reflecting	f. lampshade
7. upside down	g. overcoat
8. changeable	h. bookshelf

1. *First product name:*

features:

_____

_____

_____

benefits:

_____

_____

_____

2. *Second product name:*

features:

_____

_____

_____

benefits:

_____

_____

_____

3. *Third product name:*

features:

_____

_____

_____

benefits:

_____

_____

_____

More Workouts

• Perform this same exercise using new random combinations from the same two columns until all possibilities have been tried.

• Make your own two columns of randomly selected adjectives and nouns for subsequent exercise sessions. You may want to use slips of paper, each containing a noun or an adjective, that you can sort into two separate envelopes—nouns and adjectives. Then you can draw one slip at a time from each envelope whenever you do this exercise.

• Every now and then, try to imagine that the forced-association pair forms the name of a children's game, a Halloween costume, or a detail in a science fiction work instead of a new consumer product.

"Make it a habit to keep on the lookout for novel and interesting ideas that others have used successfully. Your idea needs to be original only in its adaptation to the problem you are working on."—Thomas A. Edison

Moments of Conception

While Dayton, Ohio, saloon proprietor James S. Ritty was taking an ocean cruise, he observed a mechanical device that counted the revolutions of the ship's propeller. It occurred to him that the same principle could be applied to counting money. He invented and patented the first cash register in 1879.

For years, George Westinghouse labored over the question of how to bring a string of railway cars to a simultaneous stop. The answer suddenly struck him one day in 1880, when he read that compressed air was being piped to drillers in mountains miles away. He decided he could pipe compressed air all along a line of cars and stop them with a single air brake.

In 1896, Humphrey O'Sullivan of Lowell, Massachusetts, used to stand on a rubber mat while he worked at a printing shop to ease the strain on his legs. When the mat was stolen by another employee, he decided to nail rubber patches to his shoe heels instead. The result was the first rubber heel.

Hubert Booth, a Londoner, attended the demonstration of a new railway-car cleaner in 1901. It worked on the principle of blowing the dirt away, and some of it blew into his face. He quickly covered his mouth with his handkerchief. Examining the soiled handkerchief later, he determined that sucking up dirt was a much more effective principle for a cleaner; so he began constructing the original vacuum cleaner.

In 1895, King C. Gillette was selling bottle caps in Boston. Absentmindedly stroking his face with a bottle cap one day, he suddenly hit on the idea of creating a thin sliver of steel for shaving that was so cheap it could be thrown away instead of sharpened. Eight years later, in 1903, he had finally worked out all the technical problems and the first safety razor appeared on the American market.

It was a hot summer day in 1905 and Elmer Ambrose Sperry was watching his child play with a spinning top. "Why does it stand up when it spins?" his child asked. Answering the question caused Sperry to come up with the idea for the gyroscope, patented in 1908, which revolutionized air and sea navigation.

In 1908, while observing his son strapping extra rubber to the wheels of his tricycle to protect them from the cobbled streets, John Dunlop, a Scottish veterinarian, was inspired to design the first pneumatic tire, with a rubber outer casing and an air-filled inner tube.

Exercise 3

Adam and the Animals: Coining Words

One of the stories I enjoy most from the Bible is the story of Adam naming the animals, a story of the first creative effort by a human being. It beautifully symbolizes the special nature of human creativity, for although Adam did not actually make the cow, the aardvark, or the orangutan, he rendered them knowable, and therefore thinkable, by giving them identifying labels.

Coining words to convey special meanings, or fashioning neologisms, is one of the most entertaining and productive ways of exercising creativity. It not only causes us to synthesize our impressions, associations, and understandings of the phenomenon we are naming, but also gives us a hook for collecting and defining more information about it.

Physicians of both the mind and the body, who are used to making up neologisms to label new discoveries, frequently encourage their patients to do the same in regard to their symptoms. Discussing what such terms mean to a patient helps the physician understand what that patient is feeling.

Suppose, for instance, that a patient complains of nervousness or headaches. It is difficult to distinguish the particular sensation that is troubling the patient from the general mass of sensations, many of which are irrelevant, that are commonly linked with nervousness or headaches. If the patient labels the sensations, then both patient and doctor have a more precise guide to their possible source.

For example, maybe the patient who suffers nervousness is most concerned about what she has come to consider a "freeze-flash"—unexpected moments when she feels paralyzed and cold throughout the body. Creating a special term gives the patient a foothold in the unknown. She is less liable to confuse more common varieties of nervousness (like "nervousness about being nervous," which could be neologized as "stepshakes") with the more specific reaction that is most responsible for her anxiety.

Neologisms can be created by combining two related words (like *milkshake, toothbrush,* or *pandemonium,* the word the English poet John Milton coined from *pan,* or "all," and *demon* to name Satan's dwelling in his epic *Paradise Lost*). They can also be created by inventing a word that has the sound or feel of the thing being described (like Carl Sandburg's *sluroops* for footsteps taken in the mud), by varying the form of an associated word (like Lewis Carroll's *beamish* for the gratuitous smile of a young child), or by employing a word with a private meaning (like Bob Dylan's *mohaves* for periods of fruitless soul-searching).

Create neologisms based on the phenomena listed below. In some cases, a single neologism is sufficient. In other cases, you are given a category of phenomena, which you need to break into separate parts, giving each part its own neologism.

EXAMPLE:

A person who always smiles when saying something mean:
  an *alligaper*

Types of walking styles:

- fast and sure, as if to a specific destination: *kabonging*
- calm and steady, as if on automatic pilot: *monarching*
- slow and uncertain, as if despondent: *moondalating*
- comically jerky: *clownshoeing*
- relaxed and rambling: *huckleberrying*

1. A person who goes to a lot of workshops, rallies, and encounter groups: ⎯⎯⎯⎯⎯

⎯⎯

⎯⎯

2. Types of waiters and waitresses: ⎯⎯⎯⎯⎯⎯⎯⎯⎯⎯⎯⎯⎯⎯⎯⎯⎯⎯⎯⎯

⎯⎯

⎯⎯

3. A day of weather that keeps you from doing anything outside: ⎯⎯⎯⎯⎯⎯⎯

⎯⎯

⎯⎯

4. Types of nighttime sleep: ⎯⎯⎯⎯⎯⎯⎯⎯⎯⎯⎯⎯⎯⎯⎯⎯⎯⎯⎯⎯⎯⎯⎯⎯

⎯⎯

⎯⎯

5. A chance event that makes you feel better: ⎯⎯⎯⎯⎯⎯⎯⎯⎯⎯⎯⎯⎯⎯⎯⎯

⎯⎯

⎯⎯

6. Types of office workers: ⎯⎯⎯⎯⎯⎯⎯⎯⎯⎯⎯⎯⎯⎯⎯⎯⎯⎯⎯⎯⎯⎯⎯⎯⎯

⎯⎯

⎯⎯

More Workouts

• Perform this same exercise, creating neologisms for any item or category that you wish.

• Experiment with words created from acronyms. A popular example of such a word in common use is *snafu* (for "*s*ituation *n*ormal: *a*ll *f*ouled *u*p.") A *peto,* for example, could be a "*p*erson *e*asy *to* *o*ffend."

• Rename things. Here is a list to get you started: the United States of America; stepmother; spouse; weekend; kiss; ground; agreement.

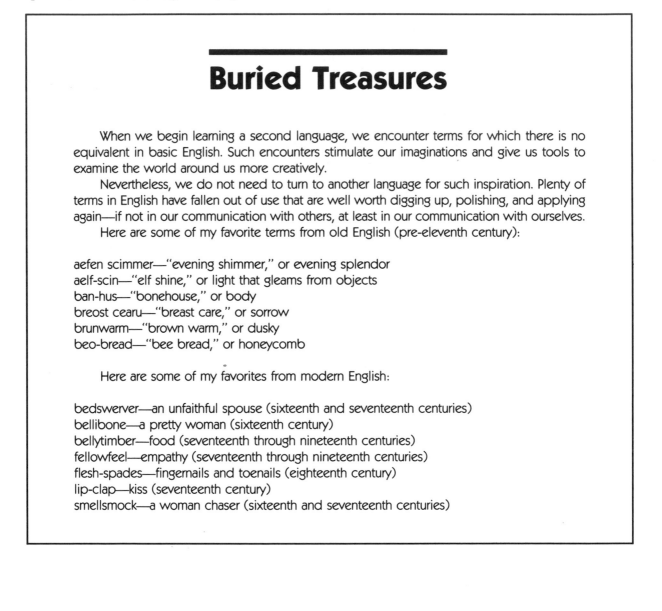

Buried Treasures

When we begin learning a second language, we encounter terms for which there is no equivalent in basic English. Such encounters stimulate our imaginations and give us tools to examine the world around us more creatively.

Nevertheless, we do not need to turn to another language for such inspiration. Plenty of terms in English have fallen out of use that are well worth digging up, polishing, and applying again—if not in our communication with others, at least in our communication with ourselves.

Here are some of my favorite terms from old English (pre-eleventh century):

aefen scimmer—"evening shimmer," or evening splendor
aelf-scin—"elf shine," or light that gleams from objects
ban-hus—"bonehouse," or body
breost cearu—"breast care," or sorrow
brunwarm—"brown warm," or dusky
beo-bread—"bee bread," or honeycomb

Here are some of my favorites from modern English:

bedswerver—an unfaithful spouse (sixteenth and seventeenth centuries)
bellibone—a pretty woman (sixteenth century)
bellytimber—food (seventeenth through nineteenth centuries)
fellowfeel—empathy (seventeenth through nineteenth centuries)
flesh-spades—fingernails and toenails (eighteenth century)
lip-clap—kiss (seventeenth century)
smellsmock—a woman chaser (sixteenth and seventeenth centuries)

"When I was a young man, I observed that nine out of ten things I did were failures. I didn't want to be a failure, so I did ten times more work."—George Bernard Shaw

Exercise 4

A Gambler in a Rowboat on Thanksgiving: Creative Writing

We are all natural creators of stories. We all spin fantasies for our own entertainment and translate our experiences into narratives that we share with our friends, families, and acquaintances. Even while we sleep, our minds develop stories in the form of dreams.

An excellent way to stimulate your overall creativity is to challenge your storytelling talent with provocative tests. Creating stories in this way prods your mind to explore all sorts of possible origins and outcomes for an event and offers you evidence of how your mind works when it is given the freedom to make up its own explanations.

Choose at random one character, one activity, and one place or time from the columns on page 166. You can do this right now, before examining the columns, by thinking up a three-digit number using only the numbers from 1 through 6. Or you can close your eyes and stab your finger at the page until you have selected one item from each column. The result will be a phrase describing a situation. Create a story that features that situation.

EXAMPLE:

situation: a king somersaulting at a funeral

story: Although his navy had conquered the remote island of Tayka-hyka during the first year of his reign, Jerzo the Fifth, king of Ahbalonia, had never visited it. The court assumed that he wisely chose not to expose his royal person to the hostile and mysterious Tayka-hykans; but in fact, Jerzo the Fifth suffered from acute seasickness and feared exposing this weakness to public ridicule. Finally, the ancient high priest of the Tayka-hykans died, and it was essential for Jerzo to attend the funeral in order to maintain his authority over the island.

The minute Jerzo stepped aboard his royal yacht, the *Maldemere,* he closeted himself in his stateroom. He never emerged during the entire voyage. Indeed, he never stood up during the entire voyage. Arriving in Woka-planka, the capital of Tayka-hyka, Jerzo was borne aloft in his royal chair to the temple where the funeral was to be held. His chair was set down before the closed bier. The new high priest-elect stepped forth, and, glaring at Jerzo, spoke these words: "It is time to reveal your right to rule by performing a secret ceremony known only to those who communicate with the gods. It is the ceremony that alone will ensure our departed high priest's passage to the sky realm of Sata-lyta."

Jerzo tried hard not to show his panic. He could not imagine what this ceremony would be. He stood up, and immediately a wave of nausea engulfed him. He keeled over and wound up somersaulting before the eyes of his horrified Ahbalonian companions. "All bow down," announced the high priest-elect. "King Jerzo the Fifth has demonstrated the cycle of change that the spirit of the departed high priest must make. He communicates with the gods and is our rightful overlord."

Character	Activity	Place or time
1. fireman	1. drawing	1. in a rowboat
2. princess	2. plotting	2. at midnight
3. banker	3. building	3. on a glacier
4. farmer	4. crying	4. on Valentine's Day
5. actress	5. exercising	5. during a hurricane
6. nun	6. gambling	6. on a bridge

situation:

_____

_____

story:

_____

_____

_____

_____

_____

_____

_____

_____

_____

_____

_____

_____

_____

_____

_____

More Workouts

• Perform this same exercise using different random combinations, until all possibilities have been tried.

• Create your own random lists of characters, activities, and places or times, and perform this exercise. You may want to write down items on individual slips of paper that can be sorted into three different envelopes, marked "characters," "activities," and "places or times." Then you can draw a slip from each envelope whenever you want to do the exercise.

> "The dynamic principle of fantasy is play, which belongs also to the child, and . . . appears to be inconsistent with the principle of serious work. But without this playing with fantasy, no creative work has ever yet come to birth."—Carl Jung

Mind Play

1. Surrealism is a game that can be played individually or in groups of two or more. To play it individually, choose the name of a famous person—living or dead—or someone you know well. Then supply answers to the following questions that best "fit" the person:

type of clothing?	type of literature?	type of color?
style of furniture?	style of painting?	type of sound?
type of food?	type of automobile?	type of smell?
type of flower?	type of television show?	any other questions
type of music?	type of movie?	involving "types" or "styles"
	type of animal?	

To play Surrealism in groups, one player thinks of a famous person or someone known to the other players and announces whether this person is living or dead. Then the other players ask whatever questions they wish of the kind listed above to try to establish the identity of the person. Guesses are permitted whenever any player feels he or she has a possible solution.

2. Express your experiences, thoughts, ideas, problems, and day or night dreams in sketches. Draw both realistic and abstract images. Make up symbols to stand for items or meanings. You may want to do a series of drawings of the same material—for example, an object or scene from various physical perspectives or several types of pictures to represent the same situation.

3. In the Superman saga, Bizarro is a parallel world in a different dimension. Everything in Bizarro is slightly askew from the way it is on earth: There are no right angles in the buildings, the people behave a bit oddly, and they wear clothes that earthlings would wear only to costume parties. Nevertheless, the overt reality in Bizarro offers insights into the covert reality of earthly life.

Invent a mythological world—a mixture of the real world in all its guises and your fantasies. Give it a name and develop a general description of the people, culture, and environment. As time goes by, think of ideas, situations, personalities, and places in terms of how they would be in your mythological world. Imagine you are writing a dictionary, encyclopedia, or scouting report of this world. What terms would the people in this world call different items? What would the subjects of various entries in the encyclopedia or scouting report be?

More Creativity Exercises

• What is the first thing that comes to mind when you hear the word *joy? Black? Girl? Sour?* If you are like most of the Nobel laureates tested by Dr. Albert Rothenberg of the Austen Riggs Center in Stockbridge, Massachusetts, you responded with opposite words: *joy/sorrow, black/white, girl/boy, sour/sweet.* Rothenberg calls this process Janusian thinking (after the Roman god Janus, who had one face pointing forward and one backward) and credits it with helping the mind remain elastic and creative. By practicing thinking in opposites, we keep ourselves from thinking in only one direction. A Janusian thinker, for example, can better express what he or she feels is true or desirable by examining more closely what he or she feels is false or undesirable.

Practice regarding things in relation to their opposites. Sometimes it is not very easy, but it can always be done. Often there is more than one right answer, depending on what you consider "opposite" to mean. What, for example, is the opposite of a house? A book? A head of lettuce? Also take a situation, a person, an experience, or an idea and try to create a word picture of its opposite.

• Synesthesia is the association of an impression from one sense category with an impression from another sense category: the sound of a smell, the color of a touch, the taste of a voice. Select some physical sensations and describe them in terms of other sense categories. Here are a few suggestions to get you started: the sound, smell, touch, and taste of blue; the color, sound, smell, and taste of pain; the touch, color, sound, and smell of bitter; the touch, color, smell, and taste of a Chopin polonaise.

• Retitle existing books, television shows, and movies. As you become more proficient, challenge yourself to create only certain types of titles: titles that begin with "where," "what," "why," "when," or "how;" titles that feature colors; titles that feature weather images.

• Rube Goldberg is most famous for his cartoons of overly elaborate and outlandish inventions for accomplishing simple everyday tasks. One invention, for example, is a device for turning on a gas burner under a pot of coffee. The would-be user, upon waking up, pulls a rope, which opens a cage door and releases a mouse, which steals cheese from a trap, which springs and pushes a rod, which turns on the gas knob, which causes a match to strike against a surface and light, which ignites the gas. Create your own Rube Goldbergs in words, pictures, or both.

• Keep a journal and regularly assign yourself creative writing projects. You can write an essay related to a subject that interests or concerns you on a particular day or a detailed character sketch of a person you encountered on a particular day or a short story based on events that happened on a particular day. From time to time, you may want to try just listing words or word arrangements, making poems, diagramming, doodling, or sketching.

• From time to time, deliberately change the way you do things. Break habits and experiment with new activities. Take a walk to a place to which you have never walked before. Read a magazine you have never read before. Do something with a friend that the two of you have never done together. Approach a job or household task in a fresh manner. Make nonjudgmental observations about the experience afterward.

Superfitness

When you feel a burning sensation in your muscles, you can tell that you have given them an effective workout, one that has tapped their full potential and will help them to become even more powerful. What is the equivalent signal in mental exercise?

The signal, of course, is not a purely physical one but neither is it a purely hypothetical or imaginary one. It is, rather, a metaphysical feeling that lies somewhere between the two. Like the symptom associated with a muscle that has been well used, the indication of a stimulated, successfully performing mind is often described in terms of light. On a practical level, we talk about a mind that can "shed light" on a situation or "illuminate" matters. Cartoonists repeatedly illustrate this by drawing a lightbulb above a human head. On an intellectual level, we talk about a mind that is "brilliant," that "shimmers," "beams," "glows," or "radiates" with intelligence. Students are described as "bright," and scholars as "beacons of knowledge." On an artistic level, we talk about a mind that is "burning with ideas" and "sparked by imagination." The poet William Butler Yeats symbolizes the creative person as one who "has a fire in his head." The ancient Greeks envisioned Apollo as the god of both the sun and the arts. In spiritual terms, we talk about a mind that is "enlightened" or possessed of an "inner light." Jesus and Buddha are each credited with saying, "I am the light," and artists throughout the ages in widely different cultures have designated spiritually gifted individuals by drawing a halo around their head.

Though regularly pursuing the *What Does Childhood Taste Like?* mental exercise program, or your own mental exercise program based on *What Does Childhood Taste Like?* you can achieve—and feel—a similar quality of mind power, not only in the context of the program itself, but also in your life, whether you are working, playing, or resting with your mind. The most complete and beneficial workout of all, however, is when you apply your mind to a self-determined, long-range, and mentally challenging project. Aiming at a particular real-world goal requires the full coordination and cooperation of all of your mental skills: flexibility, memory, analysis, decision-making, and creativity. By taking a step beyond practicing exercises to accomplishing a meaningful objective, you go beyond fitness to superfitness.

The mentally superfit person is one who puts his or her talents into action and demonstrates them through achievement. Many people who have earned renown for their intelligence or imagination are no more intelligent or imaginative than you are—a fact you can prove to yourself by considering many of the people you know well or many of the products of intelligence or imagination you observe in the world around you. Albert Einstein, the individual most commonly cited as a genius in popular surveys, was not a genius by any scholastic standards or according to his I.Q. or even in terms of any of the subjective estimates concerning his mental faculties that were made by close associates. He is considered a genius because the theories he published are highly regarded in his field. In other words, he is considered a genius not because of who he was, but because of what he did.

Life Mapping for Superfitness

In order to identify what you can do with your mind to enrich your life and the world around you, you need to do some life mapping. Life mapping involves examining all the different aspects of your life and determining which possible projects are potentially the most worthwhile, appropriate, and desirable in regard to your overall development as a productive and fulfilled human being. Here are the basic steps to follow:

1. Divide a sheet of paper into three sections. Label one section "Work" (referring to what you currently do, could do, or dream of doing to earn a living), one section "Leisure" (referring to what you do, could do, or dream of doing for entertainment and recreation), and one section "Education" (referring to what you do, could do, or dream of doing to increase your knowledge or develop your intellect).

2. Consider each category separately and jot down random notes regarding your specific interests, ambitions, and fantasies—anything you would like to do, accomplish, or have happen that falls within that category. Use whatever form of expression best suits your thoughts.

For example, under "Work," you may write "get a raise," "come up with a new idea for accounting," "public relations," "more independence." Under "Leisure," you may write "photography," "building a cabinet for my stereo," "camping out more often," "meeting in informal groups to discuss serious issues." Under "Education," you may write "reading the newspaper," "learning more about my ancestors," "a Ph.D.," "what life is really like in the Soviet Union."

3. Put an asterisk next to those items in each category that seem the most important or exciting to you.

"Capacities clamor to be used and cease their clamor only when they are well used."—Abraham Maslow

4. Review all the items you have written down under each category and identify any pair or group of items that are significantly related. Note especially any related items drawn from two or three different categories.

Assuming your paper contains the examples given above, for instance, you may decide that your ambition to "get a raise" is directly linked to your ambition to "come up with a new idea for accounting" (both under "Work"). You may also realize that your interest in public relations (under "Work") is very similar to your interest in "meeting in informal groups to discuss serious issues" (under "Leisure") and indirectly related to your interest in a topic such as "what life is really like in the Soviet Union" (under "Education").

Write down separately any clusters of related items that you can find.

5. Paying particular attention to the items you have asterisked and the clusters of related items, form two or three challenging personal goals that are specific, measurable, and have a time frame.

For example, continuing with the items listed above, you may decide that one of your goals will be "to have established within two months a regularly scheduled monthly series of meetings involving a predetermined group of well-known consumer advocates to discuss product and service issues." Another possible goal might be "to have completed an album containing old photographs of relatives and their environments, as well as self-produced current photographs of relatives and their environments by Christmas of this year."

6. Break down each goal into all the activities necessary to accomplish that goal. Consider the time each activity will take and the resources you will need, and set up an action plan tied to the calendar.

Wherever appropriate, tailor the original activities you jotted down to fit your goals. For example, reading the newspaper more purposefully and methodically could enable you to identify well-known consumer advocates or locate stories or pictures that relate to your album project. Requesting more independence in your job or arranging matters so that you have it may contribute to achieving your goal of establishing monthly meetings with consumer advocates. Researching photograph books relating to life in the Soviet Union may help you organize your album project—so might "camping out" in areas that are close to areas where your ancestors once lived or where relatives live now.

Life mapping in itself is an excellent way to exercise your mental flexibility, your memory, and your powers of analysis, decision-making, and creativity. The execution of a project inspired by life mapping does far more than provide you with exercise. By carrying through a specific commitment you have made to yourself, you not only receive a tangible reward, you also attain that intangible quality of mind that is here defined as superfitness, for you have trained your mind to take control over your life. Each different type of project you undertake involves a different type of control, and the more you experiment with the various types of projects discussed below, the more you experience firsthand the amazing potential of your mind.

"We need men who can dream of things that never were and ask why not."—George Bernard Shaw

Adding to Your Store of Knowledge

One of the easiest ways of achieving superfitness is to choose a subject that intrigues you and pursue it systematically by setting up reading programs, taking courses, attending lectures and exhibitions, participating in workshops, and/or traveling to related points of interest. Increasing your authority in a particular field will help you develop good general study habits and experience more pleasure in the company of other well-educated and self-motivated people. And since no area of human knowledge exists in a vacuum, it will inevitably lead you to a better understanding of life in general.

"I decided to begin learning Spanish shortly after I became head of my department at work," recalls Virginia Stalton, human resources director for IBM, "mainly because I didn't want to lose the intellectual energy I'd acquired after ten years of building up my professional career. I was attracted to Spanish in particular since I'd had many happy vacations in Mexico. At first I thought it might turn out to be practical in conducting business with Spanish-speaking people. But I've discovered the biggest value of knowing Spanish is that it gives me access to an entirely different mind-set. I can perceive and express things in Spanish that I was never able to perceive and express in English."

The type of surprise Stalton experienced awaits anyone who exercises his or her mind with new information. I never thought I would enjoy knowing more about politics until I began studying the art of negotiation. Approached from a different, more informed point of view, a field that I had assumed was irrelevant to my major interests—politics—was suddenly revealed as a field that could extend those interests in unique and far-reaching directions. By following political dialogues and by challenging myself to articulate political beliefs, I could sharpen my debating skills and better appreciate what motivates and antagonizes an audience.

Building Your Skills

Each of our various roles in life—worker, parent, student, friend, lover, athlete, citizen, craftsperson, public speaker—requires the repeated application of specific skills. Sustaining our enjoyment and effectiveness in these roles is a matter of continually striving to improve our performance of these skills.

Skill building is an especially satisfying way to attain superfitness because we can see ourselves progressing through three distinct stages of mental growth. First we work on identifying all the facts that pertain to a given skill, then we work on understanding the meaning of that skill in the light of those facts, and finally, we work on applying that skill. From the very beginning of our efforts, we have general goals to guide us—goals that become visibly more defined as we develop individual skills. And when we succeed in executing individual tasks more competently, the rewards are immediate and appreciable.

Many self-instructional handbooks, films, videotapes, and audiotapes exist to help you become more proficient in skills relating to a wide variety of tasks: communicating, child rearing, budgeting time, budgeting money, running small businesses, and running long marathons. You can also develop your own instructional strategies, ranging from observing role models more carefully to redesigning standard skill-practice exercises so that they are more fun.

Promoting Your Career

In the 1970s and 1980s, more and more people have put personal growth and satisfaction ahead of money and situational security when choosing how they earn a living. Some people now define a "career" as entailing numerous changes of employers and/or occupations over the course of time. On the other hand, some people have become more committed to one employer or occupation because it provides the right climate for individual expression.

Whatever the case, people have to set their own goals and devise their own ways to reach those goals if they are to succeed in today's work culture. Many organizations now offer a wide range of career development programs or counseling services. Usually, these programs and services are geared toward individual needs and objectives and are as confidential as the participant wishes them to be. Also, numerous clinics, seminars, agencies, publications, and counseling opportunities are listed in trade magazines and in library and college reference sources.

Developing a Hobby

A hobby is, in a sense, an alternative life. Whether you play tennis, collect Civil War memorabilia, cook, weave, fish, or play the fiddle, a hobby is a means of exercising all your mental talents. It provides both a support and an alternative to the rest of your life involvement in the world at large. It helps you become more curious and resourceful and links you to other self-starters who have similar enthusiasms.

One of the most famous twentieth-century advocates of developing a hobby was Winston Churchill. During the 1930s, when his political career was temporarily stalemated, Churchill took his wife's advice and turned to painting as a release for his frustrations. To his surprise, he not only loved the medium but also quickly realized he had a special talent for it, one that gained him new respect from critics and the general public. "It kept creative ideas alive that might otherwise have died for want of an outlet," Churchill claimed to a reporter shortly before his death. "And it taught me afresh the value of patience and of remaining true to one's vision."

A regular program of mental exercise can evolve into a hobby in its own right. It can also help you clarify your predilections and competencies so that you can determine which hobbies best suit your individual needs and lifestyle.

Turning a Hobby into an Enterprise

One of the most exciting and far-reaching superfitness goals is to transform a hobby into a life's work. Many famous illustrations of this exist: Colonel Sanders and his fried chicken, Grandma Moses and her sketches of farm life, John Lennon and his guitar. But one of the most inspiring stories I have encountered is that of a man who moved with his wife into my Brooklyn neighborhood two years ago from a small town in New Hampshire, ready to start a new life but entirely uncertain what direction that new life would take.

Always fascinated by dreams, Chris Hudson began keeping a regular dream journal and reading books and newsletters specializing in the subject of dreaming. His private studies, as well as a desire to make new friends, led him to join several New York City dream-work clubs, and soon he was attending a dream-work leadership seminar conducted by Dr. Montague Ullman, a classically trained psychoanalyst who has designed a world-famous method for interpersonal dream analysis based on years of research at the Maimonides Medical Center in Brooklyn. What had originated as a means of coping with loneliness quickly became a means of relating to people and assisting them experience to self-fulfillment. Today Hudson is the publisher of the *Dream Network Bulletin,* a unique twenty-page bimonthly newsletter that has captured and recorded the imagination of over two thousand dreamers in North America, Latin America, Europe, the Soviet Union, the Philippines, Australia, and New Zealand.

A beloved hobby can easily and swiftly emerge as a vocation. As you become more devoted to your hobby, the possibilities for turning your hobby into an enterprise will reveal themselves. The more prepared you are mentally to recognize these possibilities and act on them, the more likely it is that the transition will be smooth and profitable.

Breaking a Bad Habit

To break any bad habit, be it smoking, drinking, slicing a golf ball, interrupting other people's conversations, or gorging on desserts, we need to enlist all our mental powers not only to counteract patterns that are deeply ingrained and rationalized but also to formulate goals and plans that will replace these patterns with ones that are healthier, more personally satisfying, and more responsive to changing conditions in the world around us.

The trick is to plan carefully and thoughtfully to overcome a bad habit based on what you can learn about your motives for acquiring it and about the various styles in which you indulge it. Creating habit-breaking goals that are specific, measurable, and related to time is crucial to your effort; so is the invention of appropriate ceremonies and rituals to get you started on the road to appreciating and building new, more desirable habits.

Weight Watchers International, an outfit that has assisted thousands of people in adopting and enjoying more sensible eating habits, encourages all of its participants to initiate full-scale mental assessments of every aspect of their behavior. According to Dan Ebbert, a spokesperson for Weight Watchers, "Often, a client's problem is not one of overeating as such but of failing to gain sufficient satisfaction from any single eating experience, which causes that client to return to eating again and again, still 'hungry' for kicks. By improving the quality of single eating experiences, that client can more easily control the quantity of food consumed."

Overcoming Phobias

Fear of the unknown lies at the heart of all phobias: the mystery of flying spawns acrophobia; the blankness of the white page provokes writer's block; and the unforeseeable reaction of a listener triggers stuttering on the part of a speaker. The superfit person can deliver himself or herself out of such fears through education and the development of rational and imaginative strategies to induce more confident, self-reliant attitudes.

Golda Meir conquered her fear of airplane travel by taking it upon herself to rent and watch pilot-training films. By increasing her knowledge of the mechanics and procedures of flying, she became a more willing and self-assured passenger. Jack Kerouac overcame writer's block by doing what he called "wordsketching" (sitting comfortably in the midst of a particular area of the city and jotting down phrases to describe what he was observing) and "storming the typewriter" (letting his hands literally transcribe his thoughts as they came to him, without regard for where they would lead, by playing on the typewriter as a jazz soloist might play on his or her saxophone). The result was a whole new concept of prosody, which he refined and employed to produce *On the Road,* one of the groundbreaking works of twentieth-century American fiction. Adlai Stevenson, a victim of math phobia when he was in college, began collecting every game or puzzle he could that featured math and soon outgrew his negative feelings for the subject.

Numerous professional resources are available to assist people who wish to overcome life-restricting fears. But you do not have to rely solely on professional resources. The means to altering your mental response to the unknown lies ready and waiting for you in the form of any regularly pursued self-implemented mental exercise program that develops your powers of flexibility, memory, analysis, decision-making, and creativity.

Committing Oneself to Becoming More Mentally Fit

The major catalyst for achieving superfitness is your commitment to act. Between the desire to do something and the fact of doing something lies a critical gap that can only be transversed through an effort of will. The energy that a simple internal yes provides to turn your dreams and wishes into concrete acts is similar to the energy that a battery provides to enable electricity to leap across the void between the two terminals in a spark plug and set an engine into motion.

I hope reading *What Does Childhood Taste Like?* will inspire you to say, "Yes, I will take specific action to develop my mind." I know that once you make that decision, *What Does Childhood Taste Like?* will help you develop your mind in the manner that is most successful, healthy, and satisfying for you.

"Always bear in mind that your own resolution to succeed is more important than any other one thing."—Abraham Lincoln

Recommended Books About Mind Development

How to Tap into Your Own Genius, Cowan
Brain Power, Albrecht
Creative Growth Games, Raudsepp
Conceptual Blockbusting, Adams
A Source Book for Creative Thinking, Parnes and Harding
Creativity Training: Become Creative in 30 Minutes a Day, Kirst and Diekmeyer
New Think, de Bono
Problem Solving and Creativity in Individuals and Groups, Maier
Experiences in Visual Thinking, McKim
The Five-Day Course in Thinking, de Bono
The Practice of Creativity, Prince
Whole-Brain Thinking, Wonder and Donovan
The Universal Traveler, Koberg and Bagnall
60 Seconds to Mind Expansion, Cook and Davitz

Training Progress Report

After you have pursued your mental fitness program for three months, it is time to review. The questionnaire that follows is a duplicate of the one you completed before beginning your mental fitness program. Don't look at your responses to that questionnaire until you have completed this one. Then compare the two, noting progress made and areas that require further development.

Part One

For each category, circle the number next to the word or phrase that best describes your situation. Don't circle more than one number per statement. Then add up the numbers you have circled and divide the total by the number of statements completed to get your category rating. When you have finished all the categories, add up all the category ratings and divide the total by the number of categories for your mental fitness score. Estimate all totals to at least two decimal places.

Part One

Category 1

---

1. I consciously use word pictures—metaphors and analogies—to communicate more clearly:

1 rarely
2 occasionally
3 about half the time
4 most of the time
5 continually

2. I consciously use word pictures—metaphors and analogies—to make what others are communicating clearer to myself:

1 rarely
2 occasionally
3 about half the time
4 most of the time
5 continually

3. I can identify specific images that I use repeatedly when communicating with others:

1 not at all
2 with much difficulty
3 with some difficulty
4 fairly easily
5 very easily

4. I remember my nightly dreams:

1 rarely
2 occasionally
3 about half the days
4 most days
5 almost every day

5. I make a conscious effort to understand my dreams:

1 rarely
2 occasionally
3 about half the time
4 most of the time
5 continually

6. I record my experiences and/or impressions:

1 rarely
2 occasionally
3 fairly regularly
4 very often
5 almost every day

7. I can articulate my feelings:

1 not at all
2 with much difficulty
3 with some difficulty
4 fairly easily
5 very easily

SUM OF NUMBERS CIRCLED: _____
CATEGORY RATING (sum divided by 7): _____

Category 2

1. I remember my childhood:

1 very poorly
2 somewhat poorly
3 fairly well in the case of major incidents
4 fairly well in the case of most incidents
5 very vividly

2. I recall names of people and places after first exposure:

1 rarely
2 occasionally
3 about half the time
4 most of the time
5 continually

3. I use written notes to remember items:

1 continually
2 most of the time
3 about half the time
4 occasionally
5 rarely

4. I employ special tricks to remember things:

1 rarely
2 occasionally
3 about half the time
4 most of the time
5 continually

5. I use _____ special trick(s) routinely to remember things:

1 no
2 one
3 two or three
4 several
5 many

6. I find myself forgetting things on my schedule:

1 continually
2 most of the time
3 about half the time
4 occasionally
5 rarely

7. I typically recall facts about a subject:

1 in general terms
2 with a small amount of detail
3 in a fair amount of detail
4 in substantial detail
5 in very specific detail

8. I find myself looking up the same one phone number or the same one fact:

1 continually
2 most of the time
3 about half the time
4 occasionally
5 rarely

SUM OF NUMBERS CIRCLED: _____
CATEGORY RATING (sum divided by 8): _____

Category 3

1. I estimate time lengths of events:

1 very poorly
2 inaccurately most of the time
3 inaccurately about half the time
4 accurately most of the time
5 with a great degree of accuracy

2. I estimate distances between two points:

1 very poorly
2 inaccurately most of the time
3 inaccurately about half the time
4 accurately most of the time
5 with a great degree of accuracy

3. I estimate weights and sizes:

1 very poorly
2 inaccurately most of the time
3 inaccurately about half the time
4 accurately most of the time
5 with a great deal of accuracy

4. I solve puzzles and mysteries:

1 with a great deal of difficulty most of the time
2 with some degree of difficulty most of the time
3 with some degree of difficulty about half the time
4 with ease most of the time
5 with ease all of the time

5. I am able to anticipate the outcome of events:

1 rarely
2 occasionally
3 about half the time
4 most of the time
5 continually

6. I employ special tricks to analyze things:

1 rarely
2 occasionally
3 about half the time
4 most of the time
5 continually

7. I use _____ special trick(s) routinely to analyze things:

1 no
2 one
3 two or three
4 several
5 many

SUM OF NUMBERS CIRCLED: _____
CATEGORY RATING (sum divided by 7): _____

Category 4

1. I respond to crises:

1 with a great deal of failure and frustration
2 with failure and frustration most of the time
3 with failure and frustration about half the time
4 with success and comfort most of the time
5 with success and comfort all of the time

2. I formulate specific and measurable objectives for a project:

1 rarely
2 occasionally
3 about half the time
4 most of the time
5 continually

3. I establish priorities among different goals and tasks:

1 rarely
2 occasionally
3 about half the time
4 most of the time
5 continually

4. I experiment with alternatives when performing a task or achieving a goal:

1 rarely
2 occasionally
3 about half the time
4 most of the time
5 continually

5. I employ specific procedures in order to come to decisions:

1 rarely
2 occasionally
3 about half the time
4 most of the time
5 continually

6. I use _____ specific procedure(s) routinely to come to decisions:

1 no
2 one
3 two or three
4 several
5 many

7. I have trouble coming to a final decision:

1 continually
2 most of the time
3 about half the time
4 occasionally
5 rarely

SUM OF NUMBERS CIRCLED: _____
CATEGORY RATING (sum divided by 7): _____

Category 5

1. I experience what I consider to be a creative thought:

1 rarely
2 occasionally
3 fairly regularly
4 very often
5 all of the time

2. I act on the creative thoughts I experience:

1 rarely
2 occasionally
3 about half the time
4 most of the time
5 continually

3. I employ specific procedures to inspire creative thoughts:

1 rarely
2 occasionally
3 fairly regularly
4 very often
5 all of the time

4. I use _____ specific procedure(s) routinely to inspire creative thoughts:

1 no
2 one
3 two or three
4 several
5 many

5. I entertain myself in leisure moments by inventing my own activities to perform:

1 rarely
2 occasionally
3 about half the time
4 most of the time
5 continually

6. I have trouble coming up with innovative approaches to things:

1 continually
2 most of the time
3 about half the time
4 occasionally
5 rarely

SUM OF NUMBERS CIRCLED: _____

CATEGORY RATING (sum divided by 6): _____

MENTAL FITNESS SCORE (sum of category ratings divided by 5): _____

Category 1 gives a profile of your flexibility; 2, memory; 3, analytical powers; 4, decision-making skills; 5, creativity. The closer to a score of 5 you come, the more mentally fit you have rated yourself.

Part Two

Category 1: Flexibility

1. To me, "mental flexibility" means:

_____

_____

_____

_____

2. Ways in which I am mentally flexible are:

_____

_____

_____

_____

3. Ways in which I need to be more mentally flexible are:

_____

_____

_____

_____

4. Specific things I can do to develop my mental flexibility are:

_____

_____

_____

_____

Category 2: Memory

1. To me, having a good memory means:

_____

_____

_____

_____

2. Ways in which I use my memory well are:

_____

_____

_____

_____

3. Ways in which I need to use my memory more effectively are:

_____

_____

_____

_____

4. Specific things I can do to develop a better memory are:

_____

_____

_____

_____

Category 3: Analysis

1. To me, being good at analyzing things means:

_____

_____

_____

_____

2. Ways in which I analyze things well are:

_____

_____

_____

_____

3. Ways in which I need to be better in analyzing things are:

_____

_____

_____

_____

4. Specific things I can do to develop my analytical abilities are:

_____

_____

_____

_____

Category 4: Decision-making

1. To me, effective decision-making means:

_____

_____

_____

_____

2. Ways in which I am good at making decisions are:

_____

_____

_____

_____

3. Ways in which I need to become better at decision-making are:

_____

_____

_____

_____

4. Specific things I can do to develop my decision-making abilities are:

_____

_____

_____

_____

Category 5: Creativity

1. To me, "mental creativity" means:

_____

_____

_____

_____

2. Ways in which I am creative are:

_____

_____

_____

_____

3. Ways in which I need to become more creative are:

_____

_____

_____

_____

4. Specific things I can do to develop my creative abilities are:

_____

_____

_____

_____

"Every time you tear a leaf off a calendar you present a new place for new ideas and progress."—Charles F. Kettering